Mark

Abe & Esther Krah

Anybody Here Know Right from Wrong?

Bill Stearns

VICTOR BOOKS

a division of SP Publications, Inc.

WHEATON ILLINOIS 60187

Offices also in Fullerton. California • Whitby. Ontario. Canada • Amersham-on-the-Hill. Bucks. England

Seventh printing, 1982

Library of Congress Catalog Card Number: 75–31310
ISBN: 0–88207–724–4

© 1976 by SP Publications, Inc. World rights reserved
Printed in the United States of America

VICTOR BOOKS
A division of SP Publications, Inc.
P. O. Box 1825 • Wheaton, Ill. 60187

Contents

Charts and Illustrations

to
my parents

Foreword

In this book, Bill Stearns makes it clear that it is sin to know something is right to do, and not to do it (see James 4:17). Obviously, two features bounce out of this simple statement—one involves the understanding, the other refers to the will. There is the issue of knowing what is right to do, and then the obedient act of doing it.

Plenty has been written on the latter—how to submit, commit, or activate the will to *do* the right thing, but there is little available that is direct and convincing to help us deal with the tough area of *knowing* what is right.

Sure, some things are clear-cut, and the only issue left is the will to do it.

But, plenty of other issues are not clearly right or wrong, and the problem is to determine what is right so that we can activate the will in the proper direction.

Bill Stearns has given all of us an unstuffy, warm, concise, and solidly scriptural book on ethics. He forcefully delineates the divine principles for helping us to determine what is right, and offers a super-practical test for any questionable behavior.

I am grateful for it, and you will be too. It just might free you to concentrate on *doing* what is right.

John MacArthur, Jr.
Pastor, Grace Community Church
Panorama City, California

Preface

It seems we're victims of a quietly subtle rip-off as ethics and morality in our society are more and more determined by vague peer pressure, by antique adages and proverbs, or by existential guesswork. Civilization is somehow losing out in the area of right living; and it looks to me as if the mushrooming consequences of this rip-off can only be offset by a restoration of biblical ethics.

This study is a simplified treatment of the biblical system of determining right and wrong. It is by no means an exhaustive discussion of the subject. Futhermore, it does not guarantee that anyone will *do* the right once right is determined. Most important, it is not a manual of ready-made conclusions as to exactly what is right and what is wrong. It *is* a basic tool, an uncomplicated suggestion on how an individual can go on with some scriptural guidelines to answer in his own life the preplexing ethical questions of our incredible age. Simplicity does not destroy validity, but it does demand a further involvement, so you might as well plan right now on looking into biblical ethics far beyond this study. But we've got to start somewhere, right?

So what do you say we begin here with some basic thinking—so more of us *can* know right from wrong.

Bill Stearns

1
The Great Rip-off

It almost gets me down.

My typical youth-minister morning started with rain—even the day decided to be dismal—and it's progressing nicely from one hassle to the next. Small things, you know: procastinated planning overdue, late appointments, a mid-intersection escapade of running out of gas (it's raining, remember). Then a depressed mother called and cried on the phone and didn't really know why. And that hurts.

I've been getting a lot of phone calls like that lately. The topic is children, and the depressed mothers who cry on the phone have nearly-grown-up children. The particulars vary, but the situations are usually about the same. The questions come as if from a universal cue card, and the same answers are always missing:

> . . . then she moved out two months ago, and now this! I tell you, it's just so wrong! I got some of her friends to tell me where she was. Listen, she's paying $59 a month—no car, noth-

ing but a cat! And those girls she is rooming
with! I just told her that she wasn't going to
live any kind of life that way—in at 4:30, "just
watching the sunrise." Oh, certainly, I pray for
her and it just grieves me to see her throw it all
away like this. She was so active in church; we
brought her up right, and I tell her so. But it's
as if she has no sense of what is right or wrong
anymore! I guess I should just keep still, but
somebody has to keep her on the right path. I
don't know what she intends to do with the
baby . . .

So I stuff the "comfort wherewith I have been com-
forted" into the phone, suggest confidence in God,
and inwardly scream, *Too late, foolish lady!* But I
promise prayer and a meeting with the rebellious
victim, and the hopeless mother hangs up.

Problems

Things in our world seem to be falling apart. People
are feeling it—usually at home. And very often at
the crux of society's pain is this business of "youth-
problems-of-today."

It seems that youth are troubled. Youth have
always been troubled, right? But now the consequences are heavier as youth seem to set the pace
for our culture.

Everybody is aware of the "youth-problems-of-
today." The young world is experiencing hassles.
But why? Are we understanding what's happening?
Almost without exception, sociologists assure us
that the troubles of our youthful society stem from a
widespread disintegration of the good old family
unit. The feeling seems to be, "Man, if you can
make it through a day unscathed at home, you can
make it *anywhere!*"

Samuel Grafton, an authority in youth trends, points out:

So organized is juvenile life today, with music lessons, language clubs, sports, and classes, that some kids of 12 are found carrying datebooks with every half hour of the week filled in. Parents themselves are busy and preoccupied, often in organizing the very activities that keep their children busy, thus making sure that hardly anybody ever gets to be with anybody else. The successful suburban father is likely to be in such demand in his town for club, committee, and board meetings that he ends up with only hearsay information about what his children are doing.

So our society is suffering. And we all are becoming aware that a substantial part of the sickness develops in the parent-child relationship. Families are dying.

Whys

Meet Bertram—regular old typical joe-youth hypothetical Bertram. Bert, part of the most influential segment of the population, feels alone and alienated —which causes problems for himself and his community. He feels alone and alienated (we're grossly generalizing, you know) as a result of a lack of purpose and security in his background. The purposelessness and insecurity can be traced to his visibly or otherwise fragmented family, where poor Bertram initially lost trust in the reasonability of his parents' authority.

They don't know what they're talkin' about! You should hear 'em yelling at each other. Then tell me how I'm supposed to trust their judgment and obey them! They don't care what's happening inside—they just want to look good.

Oh, yeah—they tell me what to do and what not
to do, what's supposed to be right and wrong,
but I wanna know *why!*

So Bertram begins ignoring his parents' authority,
and his mother begins crying over the phone to a
youth counselor.

It's an unfortunate era when parents' and govern-
ing authorities' decrees of rights and wrongs must
be countered constantly with "why?" No doubt
about it—one can build a case for God-given authority to be obeyed simply for authority's sake.

But such is not the dominant thinking among the
young. If there are legitimate standards for suggested conduct, the young world would like to
know those "whys." David Mains, minister to stu-
dents at the Chicago Circle Campus of the Univer-
sity of Illinois, says, "Today's young person is being
taught to ask questions, to probe, to seek, to wonder
why, and to not accept what seems true until it has
been proven."

The youth movement is a bit philosophic in that
it asks not "what?" or "how?" but "why?" And this
is where parents falter. They think: *In this wild,
"future shock" age, do I really know what is right
and why?*

The young person, sometime during his teen
years, makes the Great Discovery—that parents
ain't perfect. Increasingly he would like to see the
reasons behind what is allowed and what isn't, behind the do's and don'ts which are tossed at him.
Especially if the parents are inconsistent in their
own marriage relationship, or if they are proponents
of the old "do as I say not as I do" trick, the youth
demands to know why he must honor and obey
people he doesn't even respect.

The credibility gap between what is being said

and what is being backed up not only undermines the authority of Ma and Pa but also cripples subjection to *any* authority on the part of the young person. Youth who reject parental authority automatically will experience problems with school, church, and civil authorities. Usually the authority-rejection situation revolves around the area of rights and wrongs—we do this, and we don't do that.

Let's look again at Bertram, age 16, enjoying a family discussion:

"You're not running around with those fellows anymore."

"So what's wrong with 'em?"

"They drink, that's what's wrong!"

"So what's wrong with that? Jesus drank wine."

"Well, young man—you're not! And that's that."

"Aw, c'mon, Ma. They're not so bad. How come I can't?"

"Because I said so—that's how come."

So Bert runs around with the guys anyhow. His mom and dad are always at work or with the church bowling league or something and don't know most of what goes on. And he drinks. The results: he finds the running around exciting and the booze nicely soporific. He again decides that his mother didn't know what she was talking about—there was no real *reason* behind what she said.

Bert now develops a pattern of determining according to his own limited experience whether questionable activities are right for him or not. So the whole family continues contributing to a great rip-off: our society's theft of solid childhood training in the most crucial aspect of living—what is right or best or good, and what is not.

But let's conclude our generalizations (and they

are generalizations). There is increasingly something rotten in Denmark—and the rest of the western world—and much of it has to do with the situation of the young. It seems generally that those entrusted with "training up a child in the way he should go" have been missing the mark. Mom with her apple pie and Father in slippers and with newspaper are confused as to when to be dogmatic and when to give in as right/wrong questions arise. Parents seem to have forgotten the principles behind their judgments of right and wrong. Few can satisfactorily tell *why* they feel something is ethical or unethical for their youth. And the failure of parents to formulate—and to communicate—a simple system of how best to live, is wreaking disastrous results in the lives of young people.

Or let's put it this way in the logical-though-subconscious thinking of American youth: "If somebody, anybody, tells me authoritatively what's right and how I'm to behave, I want to know his reasons to see if his views are valid." The implication is that if the reason isn't given or sensible, the "behaving" will not follow the authoritative direction. And that, my friends, is "what's happening."

Agree?

The Victim

But let's look at this right/wrong-confusion syndrome a little more personally. What's the individual result of this social rip-off of solid ethical training? I could tell you the whole sordid story—I think I've gone over it a hundred times in my mind. But maybe I'll just let you in on the "highlights."

I'll call her Andrea, and she was a beautiful young Christian girl. Was. She sat through years of Sunday School and church services and Bible studies and outreach projects, and her bubbly Christian testimony was tough to beat. But somewhere along the line Andrea missed out on how to make decisions about what's right and what's wrong. She knew the doctrine of justification, but she couldn't figure out why "grass" could be wrong if it felt so peaceful. She won in the old junior high "sword drill contest" and sang a strong soprano in the youth choir, but later couldn't see why messing around with sex was supposed to be so harmful when she really loved the guy.

Andrea certainly had been told what was right and wrong in these areas—well, maybe it was more *implied* than *told*—but in the astounding new experiences of her early 20s, there didn't seem to be any *reasons* behind a lot of the old do's and don'ts.

And she was honestly sincere. Andrea had a deep desire to be real—to be natural and honest. And chaining herself to apparently unfounded, legalistic rules-of-conduct ("I don't see any commandment for your 'marriage ceremonies' in the Bible") wasn't being real and honest the way God reportedly wanted Christians to be.

She felt warmly wonderful on marijuana and moved quickly to speed and LSD ("There's no mention of drugs in the Bible, and if it's wrong why do you take aspirin or anesthesia or drink coffee?"), beginning to live more and more by her feelings. She loved deeply and so just lived with a guy after her first marriage fizzled on feelings after five weeks. But he left her for more welfare, and when I met with her she had just delivered his deformed "blue baby."

Andrea was slow to analyze things—her thinking obviously dulled by dope—as we kicked around the problems of living by feelings, "going by glands," determining rights and wrongs by guesswork. And when we had talked across a red formica kitchen tabletop for two hours that California afternoon, I finally thought she had understood.

But that was three years ago and I just got a letter last week mentioning the joyous news that Andrea had recently married again—after knowing the guy for a few short weeks. So now I'm wondering what I'm supposed to say when I see her, and if a person can reteach himself God's prescriptions for righteousness and the abundant life, and if Andrea will ever be a beautiful girl again.

It's not that Andrea's a threat to the defense of America. She hasn't suddenly blossomed into a national subversive. But Andrea, like millions of other youth, is losing a sense of integrity—an ability to know and choose what is best and good and right—which inevitably weakens the health of our whole society.

Sunday School Kids

Andrea's story isn't meant to be a tear-jerker. You probably know similar or sadder situations. But the point is to get you thinking about one of the most crucial and yet neglected areas of living: determining the best possible—the right—way to think, talk, and act. And we're not talking about just being a nice, straight kid—we're talking about a definite way to know what's best and what isn't, and why. We'd encounter fewer stories like Andrea's if we just knew *how* to arrive at right/wrong conclusions, and *why* particular situations are right or wrong.

Obviously the first step of getting in on God's righteous life-style is to know just what that life-style entails—what is "righteousness"? What is righteous? What is right? Just to prod your thinking,

QUESTION	RIGHT	WRONG	REASON
1. "Look. Just because my hair covers my ears doesn't mean I'm a commie or something! Let's settle it—is it wrong or right for a guy to have long-to-you hair? Really."			
2. "Well, what about it? Can I go to the movie or not? It's rated 'General' and it's a whole lot better than anything on TV. Is it all right?"			
3. "Is it right to drink six cups of coffee every day?"			
4. "Hey, I just finished **Diary of Anne Frank.** If you were hiding Jews from the Nazis, would you lie to protect them? Is that wrong?"			
5: "Oh, come on! It's 1980, not 1960! You just don't have to wear swimming suit tops to the beach anymore! It's just no big thing! And nobody even sells those old two-piece suits. Don't you see how slow Christians always were in accepting new clothes styles? First showing a kneecap was wrong, then after the world did it awhile Christians finally saw that there was nothing racy about knees. Then they finally realized that there was nothing wrong with two-piece suits. So if it'll be OK for me to go topless in another 20 years anyway, is it wrong or right now?"			
6. "Is it wrong or right for me to gamble?"			

QUESTION	RIGHT	WRONG	REASON
7. "So what about my smoking dope? It doesn't affect me in the least. Give me a reason—is it right or wrong to smoke marijuana?"			
8. "Doctor Brenton says that in my condition I should definitely be put into suspended animation for the next few years. I guess they'll freeze me just a few minutes before I will have died. I don't know if I feel right about it or not."			
9. "Hey, I was reading in the Old Testament where King David danced nearly nude before the Lord—and almost everybody else! Was he right or wrong?"			
10. "Hey, you're looking good on the televiewer! Listen, I wanted to ask you—we've never talked about it. They're about to begin developing our test tube fetus next Tuesday, and the doctor wanted to know if we wanted any genetic restructuring done. What do you imagine God thinks about something like this? Is it right or wrong?"			
11. "Now, I'm trying to be patient with you—but I wish you'd be reasonable and give me some clear-cut answers. I love the guy very much, and the fact that he's from another race doesn't bother me at all. And your "social stigmas" just aren't the same as they were. Please just tell me if it's right or wrong to marry him."			

and if nothing else your curiosity in this direction, here's a little exercise on some right/wrong questions. Simply answer "right" or "wrong" and *"why"* to the questions on pages 15 and 16. Your "why" must stand the test of biblical authority—is your reason something God scripturally agrees with? Imagine yourself as a "typical" parent:

Well, how did you do? While some of the questions were the old hackneyed (and usually still unanswered) right/wrong dilemmas we run into every day, the other questions of the present and near-future challenge realistic ethical consideration. As the "typical parent" you imagined yourself to be, you may never have to face some of the most pressing right/wrong problems that'll confront your children, and your children's children. How can you equip the next generation with ethical and moral conclusions on things you've never even imagined?

The situations weren't presented to state right or wrong conclusions. The point of the exercise was to prod your thinking to evaluate *how* you arrived at those conclusions, and *why* the situation was right or wrong. This—the how and why—is the root of the great rip-off; do we know and can we pass on a true system by which we arrive at ethical conclusions?

Along these lines, this practical study in biblical ethics is designed not to present conclusion after conclusion of what is right or wrong; but to provide the structure for understanding and passing on the how and why of arriving—at anytime, in any situation—at God-patterned right/wrong conclusions.

This is not a legalistic guidebook on how to play the righteous role. It is a study toward being circumspectly aware of how rightness is to be determined. (Unfortunately there's no magic principle that once a person does understand what is right he will automatically do it. Right?)

So let's get on with this brief study of the "hot merchandise" of the great rip-off. Let's get back to the history, bases, discovery, and use of the biblical pattern of determining right and wrong!

2
Some Huge Assumptions

Starting out as we are in search of a definite system of determining right and wrong and the best possible way to live, we're going to have to set down some pretty heavy presuppositions. With neither the time nor the space to cover the background and rationale of my three basic assumptions, I'll just ask you to "presuppose" right along with me. If it turns out that you simply can't accept one or more of these three, then forget about this study-program idea. You might as well plan on having problems in discovering God's prescriptions for enjoying life as it was designed, in being able to know and teach others rights and wrongs. The three presuppositions are just that crucial since they concern the *Author,* the *authority,* and the *ability* of right living.

The Author of Right Living
God is, and is sovereign and all-powerful.

This statement may seem ridiculously elementary to some, but the gravity of our accepting it can't be emphasized enough. First, God created truth. He designed life. And since He in sovereignty can influence the daily affairs of men, we must accept the fact that God *can* instill in our lives the characteristics of eternal truth and of life as it was originally perfectly designed. Before we get too philosophical here, let's just recognize that since a righteous God exists, the possibility of His living His righteous life in us also exists.

Second, since God rules in sovereign omniscience (He knows everything), He is the one Source in all the universe in whom the perfect knowledge of right and wrong is found. Agree? Naturally God would want to communicate this vital knowledge to the human being He has created—which brings us to our second huge assumption.

The Authority for Right Living

The authority that is to be our reference point is the inspired Scripture.

Not only is the Bible the Word of God and trustworthy throughout, it is also authoritative. Nobody seems to like the word anymore, but that doesn't alter the fact that the Bible is authoritative. What it says, goes. Period. Look at it this way: if the almighty God had crucial information about living to communicate to us, would He give a solid, definite communiqué or something that was part truth and part baloney? Personally, I can't see the sovereign God settling for anything less than the definite, authoritative truth.

Strangely enough, the Bible claims to be just that: an authoritative communication from God concerning "doing-life-up-right!" Kenneth Wuest translates 2 Timothy 3:16, "Every Scripture is God-breathed, and is profitable for teaching, for conviction, for improvement, for training with respect to righteousness, in order that the man of God may be complete, fitted out for every good work."

So we can trust the Word of God.

The Ability of Right Living
One of the things this trustworthy Bible talks about is man's total inability to attain a life-style anywhere near the fantastic level of rightness which God enjoys. In other words, even if we have an ingrained sense of what's right and what's wrong, this knowledge doesn't automatically lead to right behavior.

If you're not convinced of your inability to do right when you know what is right, I want you to try a week-long project. As honestly as possible, without giving yourself any of the old benefit-of-the-doubt, I want you to fill in the "Jeremiahgraph" on pages 22-23. We'll put it to work without going into the history of the thing's name (let's just remember that Jeremiah had some wild ups and downs in his ministry).

At the end of the seven day period, do two things. First, connect the dots with lines; second, total up all the dots' equivalent numbers for the week and divide that sum by seven. (Sounds tricky? Look, if you rated yourself 4 on Monday; then 4 on Tuesday; then 3; then 2; then 3; then another 3; and finally 4 for Sunday; add all those to get a sum of 23, which divided by seven is roughly 3.2, give or take a bit.)

Then check to see if your line of connected dots is fairly straight across at the 4 or 5 level. If not (and if you're reasonably human and honest, it probably won't be), then you will have proven to yourself that even if you seem to *know* what God wants you to do and think and say, it just doesn't seem to happen. And that's bad because it means you're not

JEREMIAHGRAPH

Beginning today, use seven days as a sample and rate yourself on a scale of 1 to 5, determining each day's "average" of how much you were in line with exactly what God wanted. Put a heavy dot under each day on the level at which you thought, spoke, and did the perfectly right things as far as God is concerned. If today is Tuesday, you'll finish the chart next Monday, and so on.

	SUN.	MON.	TUES.	WED.	THURS.	FRI.	SAT.
(5) I did everything just perfectly!							
(4) I was pretty good—nearly perfect!							

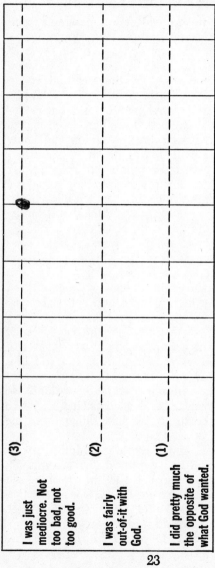

(3) I was just mediocre. Not too bad, not too good.

(2) I was fairly out-of-it with God.

(1) I did pretty much the opposite of what God wanted.

23

enjoying God's life the way it was designed to be enjoyed. Face it, you just ain't living right!

After dividing your total by seven, if you come up with an average level of about 2, it means your life probably is characterized by the fact that you're out-of-it with God. Which means you're just plain out! Or if you have something around a 3, it means you're living a generally mediocre life, which sounds pretty boring and lukewarm. (And do you know what God thinks of that? See Revelation 3:15-16.) If you come up with an average of 4 or above, either you don't need to go through this study on ethics, or you were kidding yourself when you filled in the chart each evening. (I'd tend to think that it's more likely you were kidding yourself.)

But the point is this: the "Jeremiahgraph" can help you realize that all is not right in the way you live before God. In the process of completing this project you'll discover that somehow you're missing out on what God insists is the best and right way to live.

I know what you're thinking right now. Even if you don't average 4 or 5 on the chart, you're still basically a good, all-around person. You still love your grandmother and you used to be a Cub Scout or Bluebird. After all, nobody's perfect—right? No one can expect you to be as good as God, right? So your inability to *always* do right things is no big problem, right?

Wrong! Unless you want to spend the rest of eternity as a gross, depraved human-with-all-goodness-removed. You see, God won't stand for imperfection in His presence. So if you're not perfect, you won't spend eternity with God. Which sounds pretty rough, and it is!

But our imperfection—an earthly life of hassle

and mistakes and moral pollution, and an eternal existence of separation from everything that is perfect and good and godly—has an incredible cure. The solution revolves around a "borrowed" perfection. This perfection, which we don't have but can get, enables us to begin practicing God's level of living now, and to be confidently awaiting a life with Him in eternity! That cure for man's sin is the basis for this third underlying truth that we're presupposing: the presence and control of the Spirit of God are the indispensable elements in knowing, understanding,—and most significantly—*living* life as it was designed.

Let's look at it this way. If God has the inside information on the hows and whys and goods and bads of life, wouldn't it make sense to establish a relationship with Him? Wouldn't the logical thing be to put yourself in a position where you are completely free and open to receive God's vital communiqués on right living?

So much phony propaganda and satire is tossed around concerning what the Bible speaks of as "salvation" that the whole topic seems either a superficial, hypocritical joke or a weirdly profound mystical nirvana. But it's definitely real. And it's utterly simple: God can save man *from* the life-long and eternal imperfection of sin, and can save man *to* an eternity of God-designed, God-powered living. The key to determining and living in the "right" ways is to be tied in *personally* to God. So how does this come about?

Salvation

For the benefit of any who have never clearly heard God's plan of salvation, and even for a few moldy-oldy Christians who need to be reminded of the foundation of their lives in Christ, a simple outline of this kind of Good News deserves careful study:

1. Man was created to be in union with God (Gen. 1:26-27), to be enjoying the infinite life of God Himself (John 17:3; 1 Peter 5:10).

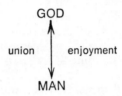

2. The first man, Adam, decided to disobey, to reject, to step out on God (Rom. 5:12). This imperfection (anything against God is imperfection) cut Adam off from communion with the perfect God; and this state of being cut off from God, of having a sinful nature, was passed down through all of Adam's race—the whole family of mankind (Rom. 3:23). The disorder, pain, confusion, and frustration of man point to this basic problem— we're separated from the One who designed us. Without God, we're empty, incomplete, and unable to fulfill our original purpose.

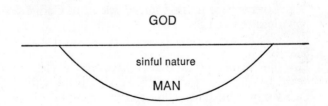

3. What's worse yet is the end result: having a sinful nature. Doing all kinds of good things doesn't erase the sin in us. The old religious trick of "balancing" off sin with good works (Rom. 3:20)—as if suddenly one morning we wake up perfect, having succeeded in pulling ourselves into perfection by imperfection—is really absurd. Finding out through mystical introspection all we can about ourselves and about God doesn't solve the basic problem of being cut off from Him by our nature either. We remain stuck with our old sin nature, which is alienated from God. So, as we physically die and miss the last chance to do anything about the problem, we send ourselves into an eternity of remaining cut off from God (Heb. 9:27; Rom. 6:23). (Hell doesn't even have the luxuries of godly influences as earthly life does. Hell is definitely not the way to enjoy eternal existence.)

GOD

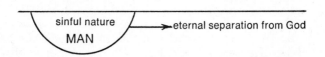

How frustrating can you get? I inherited a sinful nature that I didn't ask for in the first place; there's nothing I can do to get rid of that nature since I'm imperfect; and because of it and its consequences (sins) I'll remain cut off from God for an eternity in Hell! This sounds like *bad news!*

4. Yet God knew it would happen. He was willing to risk rejection as He gave us a choice to go His

way or our own way. It was the only arrangement that could make devotion to Him realistic. (He *could* have created man as a company of dutiful robots proclaiming, "We-love-you-God! We-love-you-God!") And so even at the scene of the first sin (Gen. 3:15), God promised a Solution—a coming One who would buy man back from sin's grasp and who would crush sin's power (Rom. 5:6-8). So Jesus Christ came to take the results—the automatic penalties—of our sins. He once-for-all as the infinite God-man, experienced all our infinite hells for us by being separated from the Father on the bloody cross of Calvary (1 John 2:2). ("Why hast Thou forsaken Me?"—Mark 15:34.)

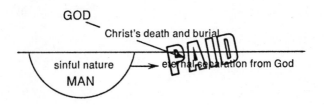

GOD

Christ's death and burial

sinful nature   eternal separation from God
MAN

PAID

5. That's great, right? But did you notice something? Though Jesus went through the hells each of us should have to go through, the individual person is not yet united with God? Nope. Though "Christ died for the sins of the whole world" (1 John 2:2), if that's all there is to what He did for us, we're still in the same old cut-off-from-God situation since we're still trapped in our sinful natures!

But Jesus didn't simply die and waste away in the grave like so many dead-end religious leaders. He brought Himself back from the dead! (2 Cor. 5:15, 21) And so He's able—as Spirit—*to step into my life.* He, at my invitation, will come to live in me (Rev. 3:20). He, in me, is my perfection! He gives me a new divine nature which is tied in with God, which allows me to be a partaker of the very infinite life of God! (2 Peter 1:4)

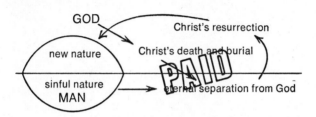

God won't force His solution of salvation on us. We, like the first Adam, still have a choice of whether we're going to go God's way or our own. And our choice rests on Jesus Christ. Will we trust in the fact of His death which paid the penalty for our sins? Will we receive Him as the Lord of our lives—the One who is going to be our Life in God? (John 1:12) The Bible puts it this way: "That if you confess with your mouth Jesus as Lord, and believe in your heart that God raised Him from the dead [after He died for you], you shall be saved" (Rom. 10:9).

Make sense?

If you've never come to the definite point of decision of receiving Christ, is there any good reason not to do just that right now?

What's the alternative? Remaining stuck in the old sinful nature for eternity—sending yourself to hell even though Jesus already paid the penalty. It's just as if you refused a pardon offered to you after you'd been convicted and sentenced for a crime—you'd rather pay it yourself even though it was already paid! Talk about a futile way to spend eternity!

And a Christless life *on earth* guarantees the same sense of futility, especially in living life the way it was designed to be lived. Being "justified" (declared righteous) in salvation is crucial to the ability of living a God-powered life.

Spirit-power
A person becomes a Christian through the work of the Spirit of God (John 3:1-8); and the Bible tells us that just as we "received Christ Jesus the Lord," we are to "so walk in Him" (Col. 2:6). Since we received Him through the ministry of the Holy Spirit, it should be obvious that we're now to walk, or have our manner of life, through the ministry of the Holy Spirit. The key not only to understanding God's prescriptions of right and wrong but also to *living* them is in our being controlled by the Spirit of God.

The Holy Spirit comes to live within a person at the moment of his spiritual birth (John 14:16-17; Rom. 8:9), when he is positionally *declared* righteous. God is interested in making that declared righteousness into a daily practicality through the indwelling Spirit. But though all Christians are indwelt by the Spirit, not all Christians allow themselves to be controlled by that Spirit. This should be pretty obvious to all avid Christian-watchers.

How is it, then, that a Christian, in whom the Spirit of God lives, can be controlled and empowered to right living by the Spirit? In essence, the process involves:

1. Confession of Sin—1 John 1:9
2. Yielding to God—Romans 6:13

In other words, when I confess my sin to God and decide to be ruled not by my old sinful nature but by my new nature (God the Spirit in me!), He controls me.

I always mistrust nice little "formulas" for being a Spirit-guided believer, so don't get the idea that a mechanical acknowledgment of these phrases of Spirit-control will transform you into a sudden Super-Christian. God works softly in lives; and He is concerned that it is our life *as a whole* which is characterized by Spirit-control rather than just a few isolated moments of dazzling spirituality. This Spirit-guided manner of life is mentioned in the Word of God as "walking in the Spirit" or "abiding in Him"; and it is here that the consistent, maturing process of the righteous life can be experienced.

Let me guess what you're thinking right now. Something like—if God the Holy Spirit can live inside me and control me, why do I need any kind of study of biblical ethics? Why not just let the Spirit nudge me along in the directions He wants me to go since He's controlling me? Good thought.

I'll throw a question at you in return: if I would allow the Holy Spirit to absolutely, perfectly, totally control me—my thoughts, my attitudes, my actions —why would any of the Bible be necessary at all? The Spirit could simply reveal to me all the history of the Old Testament, all the incidents and doctrines and teachings of the New Testament; and the Bible as a book wouldn't be needed!

The Lord seems to know our limitations, and He has not only given us His revealed Word, the Bible, but He further commands us to *study* the Bible, "handling accurately the Word of truth" (2 Tim. 2:15). We're told not to sit back and muse on the inner self which has been invaded by the Holy

Spirit but to look into the Word and let the Holy Spirit change us through *that* means (2 Cor. 3:18).

So certainly righteous living is a result of the perfect God indwelling me, but that righteous living is to be defined and determined by God's revelation, the Bible; "All Scripture is . . . profitable . . . for training in righteousness" (2 Tim. 3:16). Face it: understanding and living God's life-style of righteousness is going to require some effort in the Word on your part!

Thus the ability of right living being by the presence and control of the Spirit isn't *just* a presupposition which we must recognize in our study of biblical ethics. It's a prerequisite to living by biblical ethics.

So those are the three big assumptions on which the rest of our study will be built. Now let's get on with this great rip-off business; and begin making some progress on our civilization's theft of training in the most vital aspect of living—in discerning and experiencing what is right and best and good.

3
The Old Basics

Alasdair MacIntyre in *A Short History of Ethics* states, "To an age which, like our own, has been continually exhorted to find the solutions to its own problems in Christian morality, it will perhaps come as a relief to consider that the whole problem of Christian morality is to discover just what it *is*" (Macmillan, New York, N.Y.). Less cynical than realistic, the statement points out probably the weakest element in biblical right/wrong study: if the church is to be the divinely appointed standard-bearer of ethics and morality, why isn't it?

A Sunday School saturated youth answered a questionnaire on the topic of the New Morality this way: "I guess the whole thing isn't quite right, but I don't think badly of it either. We do need some laws like traffic and crime things, but I don't think there should be anything against free sex really. It should be left up to the people involved. Although some rules are needed against really bad free sex. I guess I really don't know." The confusion suggests immaturity, but the indecisiveness is typical of church-goers who have a vague sense of ethics and morality but who are at a loss to clearly answer new questions of ethics that confront them. And it shouldn't be this way.

Jesus Christ was firm and clear when He established the Church as the pacesetter for right living: "You are the salt of the earth; . . . you are the light of the world" (Matt. 5:13-14). But Jesus suggested the possibility of the Church losing its decay-preventing abilities: "But if the salt has become tasteless, how will *it* be made salty again?" (Matt. 5:13)

God has definite judgments of right and wrong, of what salt and light should do. But when employed by fallible men, God's right/wrong system can look as if it's lost its effective savor, as if its darkness-dispelling quality is obscured. And unfortunately this human inefficiency and obscurity is exactly what is picked up by the world as "the Christian ethic." Before reviewing the ingredients of the *true* Christian ethic, maybe we should consider the alternatives. What other right/wrong teachings has mankind endured?

The Way It Was

Mark Twain once slurred, "To be good is noble, but to show others how to be good is nobler—and not so much trouble." Which is debatable. Not that showing others right behavior is nobler, but that it's not much trouble. One ethical genius after the other has attempted through the centuries to teach mankind a basis for right and wrong. And apparently, from the number of geniuses and the wild variety of their ethical tricks, the teaching has been quite a bit of trouble. Confusing trouble.

Ethics—the system of determining right and

wrong—can be confusing because man is confusing. Whether considered mystically or scientifically, religiously or humanistically, man is a paradox of spirit vaguely wedded to flesh. He is something more than matter stuck right in the middle of a solidly material universe. The difficulty in finding a balanced approach to both the spirit and the down-to-earth flesh of men has been the story of ethical theories since the eviction notice was posted in Eden.

Plato, Aristotle, the Stoics, Epicurus, Kant, Sartre, and Bergson are the stuff of which much of ethical history is made. The myriad of right/wrong theories represented by these thinkers basically revolves around the idea that man can and should simply attach himself to an ethereal "good" which is superior to ordinary human life. To rise above the "human condition" and step onto a plane of right living, I should somehow unite myself with "happiness," or a virtue, or "pleasure," or "duty," or "liberty." In awfully general terms, I should pretend so feverishly that I live in a spiritual or invisible world that I eventually can ignore the nitty-gritty material world and its confusing conditions. All this would be great if I didn't have to figure out what honesty is in paying my taxes or what right is in settling a neighborhood dispute over someone throwing tomatoes into Mrs. Hughes' chimney.

There is another side to ethical history. Men such as Hegel, Marx, Comte, and Dewey decided that since obviously there are no superior, spiritual "goods" to which man can attach himself, the material nature of man and nature itself should be deified. Look at it this way: if mankind is nothing but a naturalistic enterprise, a simple result of the evolutionary wheel of fortune, then in order to live rightly in accordance with life's design, I should study and follow the patterns and truths of nature. This is great, *if* as an animal I can successfully ignore that other elusive ingredient of my nature, the spirit.

With the coming of our modern age, ethical thinkers began to say that since the history of ethics is so diverse, there can't be any absolute ethic. (As if because there is imperfection there can't be perfection somewhere in the scheme of the universe.) The rationale for such a conclusion has been easily pawned off on us with the help of three basic influences in our civilization: the theory of evolution, the advent of Marxism, and Freudian psychological thought.

Without killing ourselves by plowing through the grandiose scope of these influences on our ideas of right/wrong today, let's just look at the street-level conclusions gained from each. A solid evolutionary devotee must ultimately conclude that since we're all accidental animalistic beings, the only real ethic is the struggle for life, the improvement of the evolutionary individual: if it's good for me and I can get away with it, it must be right.

A Marxist fan sees socio-economic progress as his ethic: if it works, it must be right. The end justifies the means.

A Freudian freak, when ultimately isolating his ethical system, says, "If it feels good, do it."

With the weight of each of these three movements—evolution, Marxism, and Freudian psychology—saturating our outlook in every area, no wonder the typical joe wrestles with right/wrong questions: "Let's see. It'll get me ahead so it must be all right, but it's cutting the throats of my friends so it must be wrong, but it sure would feel great to me so maybe it's right after all—and anyway it's all relative, isn't it?

The only influence more ambiguous than these contemporary Big Three is their philosophical wonderchild, *existentialism*.

The Old Story

With existentialism, man has finally thought himself into a position he's been drooling over for hundreds of years—he can think of himself as his own god. He can see himself as *the one* to decide, to know what's best, to set limits or liberties. In relation to our consideration of ethical systems, existentialism—since it rejects theoretical ethics—is prime territory for an heroic attempt at meeting the spiritual/practical problem of right/wrong. And undoubtedly the most heroic attempt in our century comes as I, a god with no real absolutes in terms of behavior, can just hang in there with *situation ethics*.

In 1928 a German named Eberhard Grisebach suggested *Situationsethik* as The Answer to man's moral and ethical questions. Faithful to the nebulous sense of existentialist thinking, situation ethics proposed that I can do anything as long as I'm motivated by love. During World War II, Dietrich Bonhoeffer, a Lutheran pastor, furthered the situation ethics picture by publishing a treatise on why it must be right to assassinate a man such as Adolph Hitler. "The question of good is posed and is decided in the midst of each definite yet unconcluded unique and transient situation of our lives" (*Ethics*, Macmillan, New York, N.Y.).

By this approach, I don't need to figure out any systematic ethics because each situation is intrinsically unique—even the precepts observed and suggested in the life of Jesus Christ were simply illustrations of how love was defined in His day.

Bishop John A. T. Robinson and Joseph Fletcher in recent years have capitalized on the situation ethics game by—before throwing their hands up and prescribing an on-the-spot decision of "love"— bringing up some of the notorious sticky situations of right/wrong:

> At the Battle of the Bulge, a German infantry-man named Bergmeier was captured and taken into a prisoner of war camp in Wales. Later, his wife, compelled to forage for food for their three children, was picked up by a Soviet patrol. Before she could get word back to them, she was sent off to a prison camp in the Ukraine.
>
> Within a few months, Bergmeier was released and upon return to Berlin began the search for his family. He found Paul, who was 10, and Ilse, who was 12, in a Russian detention school. Their 15-year-old brother, Hans, was found hiding in a cellar. But they searched in vain for some word of their mother. Her whereabouts remained a mystery. During those agonizing months of heartache, hunger, and fear, they needed their mother to reknit them as a family.
>
> Meanwhile in the Ukraine, Mrs. Bergmeier learned through a sympathetic commandant that her husband and children were together in Berlin and were desperately trying to find her. But the Russian rules would allow her release for only two reasons: (1) an illness requiring medical care beyond the camp facilities, in which case she would be sent to a Soviet hospital elsewhere, and (2) pregnancy, in which case she would be returned to Germany as a liability.

She wrestled with the alternatives and finally asked a friendly camp guard to impregnate her. When her condition was medically verified, she was immediately returned to Berlin and to her family. They welcomed her with open arms even when she told them how she managed it. When little Dietrich was born, they especially loved him, feeling that he had done what no one else could do—bring the family back together.

(Quoted from *The New Morality: A Christian Solution,* William S. Banowsky. Copyright 1968 Campus Evangelism, p. 1.)

Now, since this self-sacrificing act of adultery was obviously motivated by the woman's love for her family, wasn't her action right? Wasn't it the loving thing to do? Apparently as long as she was motivated by love, Mrs. Bergmeier could have gone further—stealing, lying, perhaps even killing since it was all for the love of her family. How far could such a situation go before any of the actions became wrong? With situational ethics, who's to say? Mrs. Bergmeier and the rest of us should just hang in there and *love*—everything will come out all right then. Or will it?

All Ya Need Is Love (?)

"Yeah, we live by love. So how do you like *them* apples?"

I nodded. I had just been discharged from Uncle Sam's Army and was still enjoying as a souvenir the famous GI onionhead haircut when I was invited to visit a communal farm near Eugene, Oregon. Feeling a little out of context with my spanky-clean, all-American dress greens and clean-cut head, I tried to blend into the long-hair atmosphere of the place by asking my "guide" if there were rules of conduct within the commune's social structure.

His reply was, "We live by love." He went on to explain, "We figure that if we use love as our guideline, we'll always be doing the right thing, you know! If we love each other, we won't do anything to hurt each other. And if we love ourselves, we won't do anything wrong to our own bodies. Right? So how do you like *them* apples?"

Well, I couldn't quite figure what "them apples" had to do with it, but I did agree that the guy was on the right track. Now before you panic at the idea that "all ya need is love" in order to live properly, let's see what God says about it.

> "Teacher, which is the great commandment in the Law?" And He said to him, " 'You shall love the Lord your God with all your heart, and with all your soul, and with all your mind.' This is the great and foremost commandment. And a second is like it, 'You shall love your neighbor as yourself.' On these two commandments depend the whole Law and the Prophets."
>
> —Matthew 22:36-40

> Owe nothing to anyone except to love one another, for he who loves his neighbor has fulfilled the law. For this, "You shall not commit adultery, you shall not murder, you shall not steal, you shall not covet," and if there is any other commandment, it is summed up in this saying, "You shall love your neighbor as yourself." Love does no wrong to a neighbor; love therefore is the fulfillment of the law.
>
> —Romans 13:8-10

For the whole law is fulfilled in one word, in the statement, "You shall love your neighbor as yourself." —Galatians 5:14

Now, *you* can say whatever you want, and *I* can say whatever I want; but *God* says very plainly that love fulfills all of the laws and rules and commandments. It's pretty obvious that if a person were loving God perfectly and properly, he would never do, think, or say anything contrary to what God wished. And if a person were loving his fellow man perfectly and properly, he would never do, think or say anything which would harm or go against his fellow man. *And* if a person were loving himself perfectly and properly, he would never allow his mind or body to be polluted or harmed.

If a person were loving perfectly and properly in these three directions, toward God, others, and himself—he would then be living properly, living the best possible life. He would always be doing and thinking and saying the right things. This is easily the prime ingredient of God's prescription for right living: LOVE.

But I think you're catching the problem involved in concentrating on love as the sole guide to right living. Let's go back to my enthralling post-army story:

My commune farm guide looked so smug with his explanation of communal ethics that I just had to hit him over the head with, "That's great—living by love. But, uh, maybe you could tell me just exactly what *is* love?"

He rolled his eyes, pinched at his mustache, then very condescendingly began to drone on about caring and not offending and supplying needs and all sorts of vague stuff.

When he finally realized he wasn't really answering the question, I whacked him with, "Well, good. Uh, do you know *how* to love in every situation? And before you answer that, tell me—*do* you love others, all of them? Do you really, practically love yourself in the proper way?" (I figured I'd bombed him enough as it was, so I didn't ask the last question: "And since you obviously don't want to wrong the Creator of the universe, do you love God perfectly and consistently?")

Just about that time two of the children on the farm shrieked by the side of the barn, ferociously beating the pie out of each other. Soon the respective mothers were hovering over the melee, glaring at each other; and eventually the whole barnyard was teeming with anything but a perfect and proper sense of love.

I think my guide was catching the point: perfect, three-directional love—toward God, others, and self—just doesn't come naturally!

Now you're thinking: but that's just with "them unsociable drop-out-type rascals"; real Christians know what love is and how to love! While it's true that Christians have the potential of practical love "because the love of God has been poured out within our hearts" (Rom. 5:5), a typical church business meeting or a friendly Christian gossip session will remind you that Christians don't always appropriate in practical ways their God-given potential. So the problem is obvious. No one practices consistent, perfect, three-directional love. And so no one practices perfect living (Rom. 3:10-12). It's just that simple. Face it, we as a human race just don't seem to know how to handle this thing of loving!

So here is where we can listen to God, since He

knows just exactly what love is and how to express it in any situation.

Law

Because we don't love in perfect justice and purity, God has given us guidelines—rules of action—to love by. The Apostle John says that "loving God means obeying His commands, and these commands of His are not burdensome" (1 John 5:3, PH). Again he says, "Real love means obeying the Father's orders, and you have known from the beginning that you must live in obedience to Him" (2 John 5, PH). Did you catch that? His laws, commands, guidelines—call them what you will—form our official "manual" on three-directional loving. By obeying the manual, we're loving; and by loving we're obeying the manual! This is the second element of the biblical code of living: LAW.

Let's be certain we're understanding this. God's commands involve man's three areas of relationship: his relationship to God ("You shall have no other gods before Me," Ex. 20:3), his relationship to others ("Give preference to one another in honor," Rom. 12:10), and his relationship to himself ("Set your mind on the things above," Col. 3:2). God, knowing perfectly well how inadequate we are, has given a complete set of practical, explicit methods of loving properly in those three relationships.

God's commands concerning Himself teach us in practical ways how to love Him. His rules and principles concerning others give us the methodology for loving others. And His commandments concerning us as individuals tell us how to love and care for our own bodies, souls, and spirits. "Real love means obeying the Father's orders."

These orders, what we'll call generally "Law," are eternally "good" and "holy" (Rom. 7:12). God's laws have always been good and just and holy, always will be, and always will demand a response of obedience.

Often we become confused here as we wonder which commandments we are to obey and which we are to ignore as pertaining only to the Old Testament Jewish nation. If God's commands are guidelines to right loving and living, should we as New Testament Christians be subjected to a mandatory circumcision ceremony or an abstinence from pork?

Of course, the Apostle Paul has already answered these questions for us (Rom. 3:1 and Gal. 5:2-4; or Rom. 14 and 1 Cor. 8). But if Christians are to ignore these particular Old Testament mandates, should we also ignore "You shall have no other gods before Me," or "Honor your father and your mother"?

If not, how do we tell which Old Testament laws apply to us and which don't?

It's just this simple: if the command is confirmed by God in the writings of the New Testament, it's for us. For example, we find no paralleling principle in the New Testament which confirms this law: "You shall make yourself tassels on the four corners of your garment with which you cover yourself" (Deut. 22:12). This instruction was intended for the Old Testament Jews only. However, "You shall have no other gods before Me" is clearly confirmed in the New Testament (1 Cor. 8:4-6, Luke 10:27-28), so this is an injunction which applies regardless of time period.

Yes, folks, contrary to very popular Christian opinion, law *does* have a place in our lives! Law has no place in attaining our salvation ("Because by the works of the Law no flesh will be justified" —Rom. 3:20), but a place in our behavior as guidelines for righteous living.

But we run into problems here. I think you're realizing that there is a tremendous danger in recognizing God's mandates and attempting to live them solely to the letter. The danger is legalism—a fleshly adherence to a code of conduct. Now if God's laws are guidelines to loving, how can we be sure our obedience truly is love, not legalism? And, second, there's a problem here because obviously the Bible doesn't list every activity in the universe. What about the areas which the commands don't cover? The answer to the questions of legalism and uncertainty is seen in yet another "ingredient" in God's system of ethics: LIBERTY.

Liberty

In several passages, the Bible speaks of the "glorious liberty of the children of God" (Rom. 8:21):

- "Now the Lord is the Spirit; and where the Spirit of the Lord is, there is liberty" (2 Cor. 3:17).
- "It was for freedom that Christ set us free; therefore keep standing firm and do not be subject again to a yoke of slavery" (Gal. 5:1).
- "But one who looks intently at the perfect law, the law of liberty, and abides by it, not having become a forgetful hearer but an effectual doer, this man shall be blessed in what he does" (James 1:25).
- "But take care lest this liberty of yours somehow become a stumbling block to the weak" (1 Cor. 8:9).

So we believers—whom God indwells and controls—exist in an unusual dimension of freedom; for when God says we're free, *we are free* (John 8:36). Free to finally do the will of God, a freedom of which the unbeliever knows nothing. We are free to act and think and speak in liberty, apart from the restraints and procedures of Old Testament life. We're no longer held to the impossible task of making ourselves righteous before God by keeping the law. Instead we know "righteousness by faith." We can know the liberty of approaching the Law of God not for a stab at salvation—the Law was never intended for that (Gal. 3:23-25)—but for genuine instruction in the enjoyment of right living.

So our liberty in Christ has brought us out from under the curse of the Law (Gal. 3:13), a concept which thwarts dry legalism since we don't gain or keep our spirituality by following a set of do's and don'ts. And at the same time our liberty guarantees that, when the commands and principles of Scripture are not being violated (the old "what-about-areas-not-mentioned" question), we are completely free in our conduct. (You notice I said "when the commands and principles are not being violated.")

But maybe you're getting confused. This thing of figuring out rights and wrongs was supposed to be simple business and here we are thrashing around in the intricate areas of law and liberty and love! Patience. We'll soon finish off the broad generalities and get down to specifics. OK? The generalities in God's system of right/wrong focus in three areas: love, law, and liberty. All three are crucial elements in the biblical system of ethics, but we're not to live according to the dictates of any *one* of them. Let's illustrate:

When love is isolated as the rule of life, it becomes lust.

When law is isolated as the rule of life, it becomes legalism.

When liberty is isolated as the rule of life, it becomes license.

All three elements must interact; with love as the motive for our Christian living, God's laws as the method, and liberty as the milieu in which we act. The idea of this is seen in Titus 2:11-13; Galatians 5:13, and Romans 6:22.

Grays

> Today there is no day or night,
> Today there is no wrong or right.
> Today there is no black or white—
> Only shades of gray,
> Only shades of gray.

This chorus from a mid-'60s rock song probably expresses the philosophy of most people today— regardless of their age. There are rights and wrongs to which most of our society's members give nominal adherence. But between these white rights and black wrongs is a wild wasteland of gray, a no-man's land of situations which supposedly aren't right, but they're not really wrong either. And besides, who's to say?

It's expected that Christians would have a more definite outlook on this gray area than the run-of-the-mill Joe, but generally you'll find Christians are just as confused as unbelievers.

In a parents' seminar, I tossed out a few sample gray area questions at which parents usually begin scratching their heads. Here's what I gave them:

Using the biblical system of rights and wrongs— the principle of liberty limited by love and guided by law—answer the following:

a. "Harvey got a new heavy-rock album by the Electric Flea. Can I buy one too?"

Answer: _____

Biblical reason: _____

b. "Harvey asked if I could go to the Electric Flea light show at the coliseum—can I go?"

Answer: _____

Biblical reason: _____

c. (Girl speaking) "There's a guy from school who wants to come over and work on some homework with me, then go out for a coke. He's not a Christian. Is it OK?"

Answer: _____

Biblical reason: _____

In nearly every case the parents had a quick answer. But with further discussion and digging, we discovered that the quick answers—whether "right" or "wrong"—were vaguely justified, seldom concretely biblical.

The discussion finally centered on, "What do we follow when the Bible doesn't explicitly mention what we're facing?" The solution was then easily seen in the far-reaching *principles* expounded in the Bible. But what if a principle doesn't really seem to apply? Or it isn't clear? What then?

During the seminar, I didn't have to look far for a parent frowning with this dilemma. Evelyn's lanky son was a "good boy." Sunday School variety. But around his 14th birthday, the lousy kid began balking at Dad's homegrown haircuts. Needless to say, the 14-year-old thought he looked fantastic as the fuzzy stuff began sticking out over his ears, but Evelyn had other ideas. She and her husband finally organized to solve the situation with a solemn reading of the "hair" verse, 1 Corinthians 11:14; to which the well-prompted-by-peers youth replied, "But, Dad, how long is 'long'?" And there they were, right back in the good old gray area!

Let's try to pin some of this gray matter down. If the way God wants us to live—rights and wrongs and the best ways of living—are enveloped in some kind of pattern involving love and law and liberty, where do we find the remedy for these puzzling "gray" situations?

The motive prompting us to godly lives doesn't change from situation to situation. *Love* should be the motivation regardless of the complexity of the circumstance. Nor does the milieu, the environment of our conduct, ever vary. We as believers are free with the constant, solid liberty of Christ. So all this leaves just one element of the biblical pattern as a variable in which the confusion of the gray areas can "rip off" our understanding of right and wrong: LAW.

Now hopefully you're thinking: *but the Law isn't variable. When it says "Do not steal" it means simply don't steal, right?*

Right. The guidelines, the commands of God never change. But unfortunately our knowledge and understanding and use of them has changed. We've been forgetting what God ordered, not acknowledging why He ordered as He did, and not passing on from generation to generation the "how-to's" of these precepts of right living.

Scripture states:

You shall therefore impress these words of Mine on your heart and on your soul; and you shall bind them as a sign on your hand, and they shall be as frontals on your forehead. And you shall teach them to your sons, talking of them when you sit in the house and when you walk along the road and when you lie down and when you rise up. And you shall write them on the doorposts of your house and on your gates, so that your days and the days of your sons may be multiplied in the land which the Lord swore to your fathers to give them, as long as the heavens remain above the earth (Deut. 11:18-21).

The remedy for puzzling "gray" situations is learning how to apply basic principles of Scripture. It is these principles—introduced in the next two chapters—that we've failed to pass on from generation to generation.

4
The Principle
of the Thing

I'm being kind, but Jeff was a slob. He constantly knocked his parents, earned a scummy reputation with any girls he took out, and generally was a lazy, sloppy, conceited lamebrain. But when he enlisted in the United States Marines and considered the question of whether he would be breaking God's Law by using his M-16 rifle, one day he suddenly wised-up, and sought some counsel. He stretched out with his cowboy boots hanging on the edge of my desk.

I tried to be tricky right off the bat with, "Well, Jeff. How come you don't want to kill anybody?"

He quit picking his fingernails long enough to give me a you're-dumber-than-I-thought look, then easily replied, " 'Thou shall not kill'—right?"

"Ah, very good. And that has to do specifically with murder. But before we get to that, I really want to find out why you're so all-fired concerned about breaking that one commandment when you're stepping all over some of God's other orders to you." With his bus leaving that afternoon I knew I wouldn't have much time with him and had obviously decided not to be diplomatic.

"Hey, look man. I don't drink. Don't smoke. Never killed anybody." He was counting on his fingers. "I don't swear. I ain't a doper . . . " He shrugged in puzzled innocence. "So what're you trying to accuse me of?"

"Look, Jeff. I'm not trying to accuse you of anything. Except I ought to wring your neck for kicking dirt clods all over my desk." He took his boots down. "What I *am* saying is that I wish you were as sensitive to 'Flee youthful lusts' or 'Children, obey your parents' as you are to 'Thou shalt not kill.' You're breaking God's laws when you mess around with girls just as much as when you're murdering children. One may be worse in man's estimation than the other, but you're still breaking God's Law. Right?"

I began turning to James 2:10 when he came out with just what I expected.

"But those aren't The Commandments—the Big Ten, you know? They're just kind of suggestions— that the Holy Spirit can kind of use—to kind of guide us." He paused. "Right?"

Of course, that *wasn't* right since honoring parents is one of the "Big Ten." It took a while to explain to Jeff that in any case the "suggestions" and advice and even "casually-mentioned" principles of the New Testament were just as binding, just as authoritative, just as serious as the "Big Ten" of the Old Testament. Remember one of our huge presuppositions about the Bible being God's Word throughout? That means that a phrase such as "Long for the pure milk of the Word" (1 Peter 2:2) carries the force of God's authority just as heavily as does "You shall not make for yourself an idol"

(Ex. 20:4). And like the commandments, the principles of Scripture are of an eternal nature, for God's Word will "not pass away" (Matt. 24:35). In other words, the infinite source of these inspired principles and "suggestions" ensures the relevancy of their application regardless of circumstance, historical period, society, or whatever.

So here's where a dry old study of biblical ethics can get exciting as we get into a quick look at the principles of God's system of right/wrong, and at the infinitely-practical, nitty-gritty *use* of them!

Heavy

The *Principle of Excess* is the first guideline we'll consider as we see the practicalities of God's ethical system. (Obviously, since we're not intending this study as an academic treatise expounding every facet of biblical ethics, we're going to have to simplify and generalize. But our study and application of biblical principles will be valid—and most practical!)

The principle of excess is observable in: "Therefore, since we have so great a cloud of witnesses surrounding us, let us also lay aside every encumbrance, and the sin which so easily entangles us, and let us run with endurance the race that is set before us" (Heb. 12:1).

The writer of Hebrews is referring to an analogy used elsewhere in the New Testament to describe the Christian life. Imagine a huge coliseum-style grandstand, a well-marked cinder track, the taut muscles of a sprinter as he kneels into the starting position. The Apostle Paul says that the Christian life is like that—like a race (1 Cor. 9:24-27).

Now if we're in a race, what's the goal? What's the winner's "prize" Paul talks about? Scripture indicates that our goal in this wild race is nothing less fantastic than being "conformed to the image" of Jesus Christ! (Rom. 8:29) Got that so far? We as born-again believers are in a race. We're making progress all through our Christian lives here on earth. Some are making pretty slow progress; but nevertheless God says that we're in this race till we reach the "finish line" of being like Jesus Christ—which obviously is going to happen only as we step into the realm of heaven itself.

All right. Hebrews 12:1, then, contains an expression of the logical principle which every runner knows: "Don't let *nuthin'* slow you down." You want to reach the goal as quickly and as effortlessly as possible. So don't allow any excess weight to encumber you in your running.

When I was in high school, for some unbelievable reason I went out for the glamorous sport of cross-country. In practice we ran in soft sand. We ran up flights of stairs. We ran with teammates on our backs. We ran with nice little weights strapped to our ankles. We ran against the wind. But when the time came for the real thing—the race itself, when butterflies in the stomach signaled the start of the real competition, we ran with the very lightest uniform and shoes possible. No weights. No extra loads on our backs.

But then there was Dawson. Every team has a Dawson, you know; and this one thought he was a cowboy. The guy had a good heart—the brain was a little weak, but he tried. Anyway, one of our cross-country meets was in Salinas, California. I still remember walking the course, noticing the direction of the chilly wind, listening to Dawson yelling that someone had stolen his shoes. And I'll never forget lining up in the pack at the starting line, concentrating on my breathing, diving forward at the gun, *and running over Dawson!*

He had scarcely moved when the race started, and it took me a full minute to get him back on his feet after I plowed into him. As I helped him up, it was obvious why he wasn't running well. It had something to do with his 80-pound, chunky-heeled cowboy boots. And Dawson didn't win the race.

Now, how obvious is it to *you* when you're letting weights slow you down in your race to become like Jesus Christ? Are you some kind of a spiritual Dawson? Listen, just as a sprinter in a physical race would never run with any excess baggage, so a runner in this spiritual "race" is nothing but foolish to carry along anything that would slow him down. Right?

A weight can be a habit which takes your eyes off the "finish-line." A weight can be a "friend" who entices you off the racecourse. A weight can be an ambition that steals your vital time and energy away from the race. A weight can be virtually anything which slows you down from becoming like Jesus Christ.

How do you use this *Principle of Excess?* Let's look at a few more biblical principles before we see exactly how to put this guideline to work.

Useful

A second vital guideline in God's system of right and wrong is the *Principle of Expedience.* "All things are lawful for me, but not all things are profitable" (1 Cor. 6:12). We Christians are famous for testifying to the definite "purpose" we've found in life because of the reality of Christ. But we often fail to understand the practicality of that purpose. It's like this: everything I do as a Christian should contribute in some way to the overall purpose which God has for my life. If something—be it an activity, some form of entertainment, a personal attitude, or whatever—doesn't fit in, if it isn't expedient or *useful* toward that purpose, then it doesn't have a place in my life. Let's illustrate.

I used to be a boob-tube addict as a kid. I watched TV for hours: Captain Kangaroo and crackly old movies and cartoons and all kinds of great stuff. My eyes were chronically bloodshot and my skin pasty-white, yet I loved every minute of television.

At a definite point in my life, I recognized that God *probably* had something better for me to do each day than to sit in front of the TV. Much as I hated to admit it, those daily hours of useless viewing could easily be spent in doing my neglected homework, or reading the Bible, or other profitable, *useful* things that I never seemed to have time for.

But let's say that I still spent hours each day staring at the TV. I could defend my action (action?) on the grounds that I *could* be doing something worse instead; but I'd have to admit I was cheating on the priority items of God's purpose for my life, wasting time on something that wasn't crucial in respect to what God wanted me doing. I'd be violating the *Principle of Expedience*.

Control

Ah, yes. Here's a rich one. "All things are lawful for me, but I will not be mastered by anything" (1 Cor. 6:12b). Is something going to enslave me if I engage in it? Who or what is in the position of control? When I as a Spirit-controlled believer allow something other than the Holy Spirit to control any part of me—my mind, body, emotions, perspective, ambitions, will—I'm violating the *Principle of En-slavement.*

Working with a youth group in a certain church, I tried to gauge the kids on the "uptight-straight-loose-superloose" scale of moral standards. As a general group, they came up "confused." The kids were bitterly embroiled in, among other things, a wild feud concerning the old all-American sport of dancing. "Why can't we have church dances? Just 'cause the old people don't like the music." And the comments inevitably wound up with, "So what's wrong with dancing, anyway? Must be something, huh?"

Rather than plowing through a majestic study of Christian ethics right then and there to help them clarify their stand on the issue, I decided I'd choose just one dance-loving guinea pig for an interview. I asked him to read 1 Corinthians 6:12b, then discussed with him just what it meant. The rest of the mob watched from the edges of their chairs.

Then I asked the dancing guinea pig, "OK, being as honest as you can, when you're dancing with some beautiful, ravishing young thing, is it hard or easy to control your thoughts as a Spirit-guided Christian?"

"Kinda hard, I guess."

"Kind of hard?"

"Well . . . , really hard."

"Why is it hard for you to control your brain during those times?" I was beginning to feel like Perry Mason.

The poor guy was starting to get embarrassed. "Uh, I don't know."

"Oh, come on, now."

"Well, when you're just watchin' her during the fast stuff, you know; and, uh, when you're just kind of leaning into her and holding her on the slow things; uh . . . " He finally finished with, "Aw, c'mon, man! You know what that does to you!"

"Does the girl usually know that you're using her that way? To give you some racy sensual kicks?"

He obviously wanted to fade back into the group. "Nope. Probably not."

· "And when your mind gets rolling like that when you're dancing, who or what is in control?"

He'd obviously never thought about it before in those terms, and it was some time before he decided that probably it was old all-American lust that caused him to enjoy the old all-American dance bit. His Spirit-indwelt will wasn't at all in control at those times. For *him,* lust usually was in the position of command.

That wasn't *everyone's* conclusion however. For instance, it was obvious that most of the girls didn't view their interest in dancing in the same way. But with the new insight from the Enslavement Principle, the girls too were suddenly a little more hesitant to defend the pastime as being *thoroughly* innocent.

Selling out to any ungodly influence is a violation of the *Principle of Enslavement.*

Example

One famous guideline of the New Testament is often, unfortunately, the only principle some Christians use—the Principle of Example. All sorts of biblical passages (1 Cor. 8:1-13; Rom. 14:13-23; 15:1-3; 1 Cor. 10:23) focus on the practicalities of this guideline for determining rights and wrongs. It can be understood in several different ways—in terms of the unity of the body of Christ, in terms of the maturing process of sanctification in the believer, in terms of individual freedoms in Christianity. But for the sake of clarity, let's go back to our analogy of the Christian life being compared to a race.

Just as I am to be thoroughly involved in my race for the goal of becoming conformed to the image of Christ, my brothers and sisters in Christ (we're all in the same Family now according to John 1:12) are likewise running. Some are running faster than I, some more slowly. But we're all running in this thing together. We're all on the same team. Now what kind of clod would do some weird footwork that would trip up his teammate, right in the thick of a championship race? (You're right, I guess there always could be a Dawson in the crowd.) But certainly a runner wouldn't intentionally cause a teammate to stumble in his race.

So why are we so callous in the spiritual realm, often completely ignoring the plight of our stumbling brothers in Christ? That all sounds so terribly cruel that I'm sure you're thinking, *Oh, but I'd never do that!* I'm afraid that's what most all of us Christians would say. And yet we see, throughout the Family of God, Christian after Christian sprawled all over the racecourse as a result of some other runner's violation of the *Principle of Example*.

The annual church youth-mob winter retreat provides the ideal stage for an Example Principle "Trip":

> *Setting: Interior of a dimly-lit, jostling church bus. Center-stage focus on three principal characters: Derric and Lisa huddled together, a blanket around their shoulders; and John seated alone behind them.*
>
> *Derric (over his shoulder):* Hey, John. Didja learn a lot this weekend?

> *John (nodding):* Never heard most of the Old
> Testament stuff before.
>
> *Derric:* Well, if I can help you with, you know,
> questions or something, let me know, OK?
>
> *John:* It's a deal.
>
> *Derric turns back to converse with Lisa, huddling
> more closely under the blanket to talk about the
> spiritual implications of the retreat. John sits back
> quickly, misreading the couple's actions as some-
> thing less than innocent; and determines his
> future standards of co-ed travel in the church
> bus. None of the characters is aware of a slowly-
> descending placard appearing down-stage. The
> sign reads "The Trip."*

Corny but typical, the situation sees a Christian
couple violating the Example Principle while a
brother in Christ is tripped up in his race to become
more like Jesus Christ.

Exam Time

Well, we're finally getting down to the meat of all
this. But to recap some things quickly so we know
just what we're doing:

1. God knows what's right and wrong, what's loving and what isn't in the three-directional sense—
toward God, others, and self.

2. The Bible is our Official Manual for right living (and thus right loving). The three integral fac-
ets of biblical conduct are love, law or limits, and
liberty—no single factor can stand alone as the rule
of life.

3. Empowered by the Holy Spirit, the believer is
finally able to live according to God's design by
acknowledging the commands and principles of the
Bible. These are neither sources of salvation nor

sanctification, but are divine guidelines to the best possible manner of life.

4. The commands of Scripture are explicit in many areas; and where no specific direction is given, scriptural principles apply which are as authoritative and binding as the commandments themselves.

Ethical principles we've touched on so far include the principles of Excess, Expedience, Enslavement, and Example. Now let's put them to work by using the following "checklist."

CHECKLIST INSTRUCTIONS

1. After reading these concise, handy instructions, do exercises **A** and **B.** Then for **C,** pick an activity that genuinely puzzles you as to whether it is right or wrong.

2. Pray for wisdom (James 1:5) and guidance (John 16:13) from the Holy Spirit.

3. In the honesty of the Spirit, run the activity through the checklist of principles. (If you're going to "fudge" on being honest, you're obviously not going to be desirous of living a righteous life anyway, so you may as well go read the newspaper for all the good this exercise will do you!) Check under True (+) or False (−) as you answer the different principles' statements. If your questioned activity just doesn't seem to apply or register a definite true or false, simply leave that particular response blank. (Example: If my question is whether it is right or wrong for me to listen to rock music on my way to work, when I get to the statement of the Expedience Principle I may realize that the activity isn't really profitable, but then it's not necessarily detrimental either. I can't make a clear true or false, so I just leave a blank at that slot.)

4. If even a single minus appears, you know that God is saying to you personally that this activity isn't the best way for you to live. It would violate a scriptural principle in your case. It would be *wrong!* If only a string of plus marks result in your checklist, there's a healthy chance that this activity is right for you! But observe the note below as you begin the checklist.

NOTE: Three things to acknowledge here:

- Only four biblical principles appear in this checklist. That's a pretty slim representation of the total number of principles enunciated in the Bible. There are more than four principles dealing with the "gray" areas of living, so don't think that the results of this checklist will be the final say on everything!

- Some activities are amoral. They're really neither right nor wrong—like eating a banana. You are not better morally if you do or worse if you don't. In such cases, you may come up with blanks following all the principles. If that's the case with your questioned activity, then it's obvious that this activity lies openly in the realm of your Christian freedom. However, if your doctor told you "No bananas!" in order to care properly for your body, there *would* be some responses, and it would become a moral question. Right?

- Remember, if you and God don't agree on the rightness or wrongness of something, it's *your* problem—not His. Regardless of how you feel about the activity, no matter how you may try to rationalize, just trust God that He knows what He's doing. He has a habit of being right on things. So walk by faith in obedience.

Now, using the wisdom of the Spirit . . .

A. Is reading my Bible right or wrong?

REFERENCE	PRINCIPLE	TRUE	FALSE
Heb. 12:1	EXCESS: It doesn't slow me down spiritually		
1 Cor. 6:12	EXPEDIENCE: It can be profitable, useful		
1 Cor. 6:12	ENSLAVEMENT: I can be Spirit-controlled in this		
Rom. 14:13	EXAMPLE: It can allow me to be a good example		
THEREFORE READING MY BIBLE IS . . . ___RIGHT___WRONG			

B. Is getting drunk right or wrong?

REFERENCE	PRINCIPLE	TRUE	FALSE
Heb. 12:1	EXCESS: It doesn't slow me down spiritually		
1 Cor. 6:12	EXPEDIENCE: It can be profitable, useful		
1 Cor. 6:12	ENSLAVEMENT: I can be Spirit-controlled in this		
Rom. 14:13	EXAMPLE: It can allow me to be a good example		
THEREFORE GETTING DRUNK IS . . . ___RIGHT___WRONG			

C. Your own question on right/wrong.

REFERENCE	PRINCIPLE	TRUE	FALSE
Heb. 12:1	EXCESS: It doesn't slow me down spiritually		
1 Cor. 6:12	EXPEDIENCE: It can be profitable, useful		
1 Cor. 6:12	ENSLAVEMENT: I can be Spirit-controlled in this		
Rom. 14:13	EXAMPLE: It can allow me to be a good example		
THEREFORE MY QUESTIONED ACTIVITY IS . . . ___RIGHT___WRONG			

Well, how did you do? One fantastic thing about acknowledging the principles of living as set forth in the Bible, as you exercise this method of finding out what's right and what isn't, is that your sense of judgment in this area of right/wrong will grow (Heb. 5:14). Even as simple and obvious as this exercise has been, you've gained some spiritual discernment.

Someone may say, "I don't need your principles checklist to decide item **B**. Scripture plainly commands us, 'Do not get drunk with wine, for that is dissipation'" (Eph. 5:18).

Correct! And for that you get an extra star for learning the previous lesson: that law (God's Word) specifically tells us what is right and wrong in many cases.

The Reference Point

As simple as it was to make use of our four principles, maybe you're still a bit confused because it seems that the reference point—the one making the decision of right or wrong—is *you*. And isn't that the main problem with every ethical system other than Christianity? The fallible human being makes the fallible decision according to fallible information. For example, in Situation Ethics, a man determines what action is loving and what action is not; then he chooses the right—the most loving action. He bases his decision of what is right on his decision of what is loving (and who knows enough about love?) So man himself is the reference point of Situation Ethics. Sounds a bit unrealistic, doesn't it? We can say man-as-the-reference-point *is* the problem with every other ethical system. But it's not the problem with biblical ethics. Why?

Remember our huge assumptions as we started

our study? Those dramatic points on the Word of God being our authority, and on the necessity of being controlled by the Holy Spirit were mentioned not to just tickle your speed-reading abilities. These are the unique bases which make this system of determining rights and wrongs totally exclusive!

Yes, man is involved. He has to be since we're dealing with *his* life and conduct. But he isn't the reference point, the fulcrum upon which the right/wrong scale is balanced. Our reference point is the Bible with its system of principles. And our decision-maker, the one who decides how an action relates to a scriptural principle, is the Spirit of God!

Yes, you heard correctly. When a human being is "filled" (Eph. 5:18) or controlled by the Holy Spirit, when he asks for supernatural wisdom from God (James 1:5), when he is trusting the Lord to direct his paths (Prov. 3:5-6), a decision made in his mind is Spirit-guided—it's a decision authored by God Himself! A Spirit-controlled Christian actually is thinking God's thoughts, living God's life, making God's decisions!

Have you ever thought of the Christian life in those terms? If we can't trust the Holy Spirit to guide us in making a right decision which He Himself would make, then we might as well close up shop and wait for the Millennium!

So biblical ethics is not the usual process of man making a decision as to how an activity relates to the universe in general; it's the Spirit of God making a decision as to how an activity relates to the principles of the Word of God! And *that*, my friend, is exciting.

Principles Only
We seem to be talking only about biblical principles

in all this. Why not dwell more on how the explicit commandments fit into this picture of determining right and wrong? The answer is very simple.

First, if we determined right and wrong by running an activity through a checklist of explicit commandments (God's will in specific situations) *and* the principles, we'd have a checklist three miles long! (There *are* a lot of commands in the Bible!) There'd be a pretty drastic problem in the plain logistics of the process. And we'd find that since the commands *are* explicit in specific areas, *all* of them wouldn't need consideration for just one particular activity.

Then second, we're not dealing much with the definite commandments of Scripture because they're *included* in the principles of Scripture!

The commandment "You shall not steal" would be obeyed completely if a person didn't violate the principle of "with humility of mind let each of you regard one another as more important than himself" (Phil. 2:3).

The command to "honor the Lord from your wealth, and from the first of all your produce" (Prov. 3:9) is included in principles such as the Giving Principle: "But just as you abound in everything, in faith and utterance and knowledge and in all earnestness and in the love we inspired in you, see that you abound in this gracious work also" (2 Cor. 8:7). Paul further explains this inclusion idea (Rom. 13:9-10), but let's think of it in analogy: the many specific traffic regulations in our nation, the commands of "Speed Limit, 40 mph" and "Stop at all flashing railroad signals" and "Slow, pedestrian crossing," are all included in the one basic principle: "Drive safely." Make sense?

And finally, we're focusing on the scriptural prin-

ciples rather than the whole commandment structure of the Bible because it is the principles, with
their potential of infinite application (the principles
are part of the eternal Word, remember), which
are God-designed to handle the "gray" questions of
right and wrong. And it's the "gray" matter that has
our contemporary "Christian" society puzzled,
right? It's really a fairly simple matter: *whenever
the commandments apply specifically, use them.
When a commandment doesn't apply specifically,
use the principles.*

So let's focus on some more principles!

5
And the Morals of the Story

Telling It

The *Evangelism Principle* is that we always need to be considering our witness to someone who isn't a Christian. We should be concerned as to how out actions and attitudes affect unbelievers, in order to see them won to Christ (see 1 Cor. 9:19-22; 10:27-29; Col. 4:5). Most of us vaguely follow this principle. We want non-Christians to be generally impressed with the fact that there are religious people around. I'm sure they are impressed by them, but the impression is worthless unless it is purposely directed toward salvation in the Lord Jesus Christ.

Jim was the bus driver, and we, the clean-cut Christian college touring chorale, were determined to convert him by the end of the tour. We would casually run on about "spiritual things" within the hearing of our captive listener, we'd invite him to each concert, and we'd regularly pray about him. But it wasn't until someone caught Jim's reaction to the way the trash seemed to collect on the bus floor each day that we realized as a group our full responsibility to the poor guy.

We saw that the amoral habit of dropping gum wrappers—just as any other passenger group would do—was the main reason Jim was suspicious of our smooth-talking Christianity. ("You may talk a good line, but you're just like everybody else.") As a group we knew we were violating the Principle of Evangelism. A crumpled bit of trash suddenly took on right/wrong meaning as a man's spiritual destiny was being influenced. We finished the tour with a consistently clean bus floor, pockets of gum wrappers, and a born-again bus driver!

Edification

"All things are lawful, but not all things are profitable. All things are lawful, but not all things edify" (1 Cor. 10:23). Edification has to do with helpfulness, with building up other Christians. So the question which comes from the Edification Principle is this: Can this be helpful to my brother in Christ; will it teach him something beneficial about being more Christlike? While the Example Principle centered more on the thought of being a general "model" of Christlikeness to a spiritual brother, the Edification Principle involves a stronger sense of actively building up my fellow Christian. And it can be done through all kinds of means.

Take music, for example. Music, according to the Bible, will be present in heaven. It's an eternal phenomenon which can be enjoyed and used right now; and it *is* being used in many refreshing modes to edify believers. But the Christian musician who thinks he must "teach" through every song is missing the point of edification. To just reel off instruction to fellow Christians is not equivalent to building them up in Christ. Simply giving the listener opportunity to meditate on God, or to identify with an expression of spiritual sentiment can edify. Even instrumental Christian music can edify! "So then let us pursue the things which make for . . . the building up of one another" (Rom. 14:19).

Exalting

While some of the other main principles of the Word have to do with modeling godly character before the unbelieving world or before other believers, the *Exaltation Principle* is concerned with maintaining godly character before God! At first glance it may seem a little peculiar to live in a godly manner for the Lord's benefit, as if we're trying to impress Him! But remember what God instituted as the ultimate purpose of mankind? It was to be "conformed to the image of His Son" (Rom. 8:29). God wants to see Christ in us.

Are you ready for this one: God wants to see God in us! This is what the Bible indicates (Rom. 15:5-9; 1 Cor. 6:20; 10:31—"glorifying" God means to manifest the reflection of what God is like). We bring glory to God by becoming like Him. We glorify the name of God when He lives His life in us. But we're getting a little mystical here, perhaps. Let's leave the meaning of the Exaltation Principle at the idea that no thought, word, or action should mar the reflection of who God is or prevent His qualities from being developed in us.

Imitating

The old *In His Steps* idea of asking, "If Christ were in this situation, would He do this or that?" basically comes from the biblical *Principle of Emulation*. (Unfortunately most Christians refer to Robert

Shelton's novel *In His Steps* as the basis for this Christian principle more than to the Word.) Scripture declares that Christ is living His life in me (Gal. 2:20). It tells Christians to be "followers" or, literally, "imitators" of God (Eph. 5:1). It says, "The one who says he abides in Him ought himself to walk in the same manner as He walked" (1 John 2:6). So we are to live as Christ lived. The question would be: do these words or thoughts or activities enable me to emulate Jesus Christ?

Just a parenthetical thought here: imitating Christ does not mean imitating the earthly society in which Christ lived. Emulating Jesus has nothing to do with wearing Oriental robes or Palestinian sandals. There's not a thing wrong with these trappings, if you want to look like a first-century Jew (though it probably won't do a lot for the Evangelism Principle). Imitating Jesus means imitating His *manner of life,* which we find detailed in the Gospels. The apostles who wrote about Jesus' life mentioned neither His appearance nor dress, but His demeanor. He shouted against hypocrisy. He upheld government. He cared for poor people. He showed compassion to the point of tears. And it's this—His manner of life—that we are to imitate.

Exam Time
We have now outlined four more rich principles of Scripture. Using the same guidelines as before, let's run some activities through a checklist to determine what is right or wrong. Remember:

1. Ask the Spirit for wisdom and guidance, and above all, control.

2. If your questioned activity is neither true nor false with respect to one of the principles, simply leave a blank at that slot.

3. If you come up with even one "minus," the questioned activity is definitely not for you! It's wrong. If you don't agree with God, it's still your responsibility to respond as He dictates—He knows what's happening, you don't.

4. Again, these aren't all the principles of the Word. They *are* a good cross-section of the major biblical principles, so your Spirit-guided conclusions will be more accurate than in the last checklist exercise. But beware of being *too* dogmatic on the rightness or wrongness of something you've run through even this checklist. Conclusive it *ain't!*

Fill out the charts on pages 73-74, again using the wisdom of the Spirit.

Are you getting more adept at "discerning both good and evil" in all this? Even when the questioned activity is something you have already firmly decided on as right or wrong for you, the very exercise of the principles' application is a healthy factor in spiritual growth.

Questions

Undoubtedly, if you're normal, all sorts of questions are coming up in your mind as the use of the biblical system of ethics becomes a little more real to you. I was hoping that questions *would* come; since if you swallowed this clever little "checklist" idea without a bit of discomfort, it's a probable indication that you're not thinking it through elaborately enough. So let's look at some of your questions.

1. *An "Eternal" Notebook?*   Your question could be: Am I going to be forced to carry around some bulky notebook of checklists for the rest of my life?

The answer is no.

As we mentioned, Scripture says, "But solid food

A. Is movie-going right or wrong for me?

REFERENCE	PRINCIPLE	TRUE	FALSE
Heb. 12:1	EXCESS: It doesn't slow me down spiritually		
1 Cor. 6:12	EXPEDIENCE: It can be profitable, useful		
1 Cor. 6:12	ENSLAVEMENT: I can be Spirit-controlled in this		
Rom. 14:13	EXAMPLE: It can allow me to be a good example		
Col. 4:5	EVANGELISM: It can help spread the Gospel		
1 Cor. 10:23	EDIFICATION: It can help other Christians		
1 Cor. 10:31	EXALTATION: It can glorify God		
1 John 2:6	EMULATION: I can imitate Christ in this		
THEREFORE MOVIE-GOING IS . . .		___RIGHT	___WRONG

B. Is going to an "R" rated movie right or wrong for me?

REFERENCE	PRINCIPLE	TRUE	FALSE
Heb. 12:1	EXCESS: It doesn't slow me down spiritually		
1 Cor. 6:12	EXPEDIENCE: It can be profitable, useful		
1 Cor. 6:12	ENSLAVEMENT: I can be Spirit-controlled in this		
Rom. 14:13	EXAMPLE: It can allow me to be a good example		
Col. 4:5	EVANGELISM: It can help spread the Gospel		
1 Cor. 10:23	EDIFICATION: It can help other Christians		
1 Cor. 10:31	EXALTATION: It can glorify God		
1 John 2:6	EMULATION: I can imitate Christ in this		
THEREFORE GOING TO AN "R" RATED MOVIE IS . . .		___RIGHT	___WRONG

C. Your own question on right/wrong.

REFERENCE	PRINCIPLE	TRUE	FALSE
Heb. 12:1	EXCESS: It doesn't slow me down spiritually		
1 Cor. 6:12	EXPEDIENCE: It can be profitable, useful		
1 Cor. 6:12	ENSLAVEMENT: I can be Spirit-controlled in this		
Rom. 14:13	EXAMPLE: It can allow me to be a good example		
Col. 4:5	EVANGELISM: It can help spread the Gospel		
1 Cor. 10:23	EDIFICATION: It can help other Christians		
1 Cor. 10:31	EXALTATION: It can glorify God		
1 John 2:6	EMULATION: I can imitate Christ in this		
THEREFORE MY QUESTIONED ACTIVITY IS . . . ___RIGHT___WRONG			

is for the mature, who because of practice have their senses trained to discern good and evil" (Heb. 5:14). This checklist approach is only a temporary tool which enables us to consider what we should have been considering all along—the full perspective of biblical principles—in gauging our conduct. But though the checklist is a temporary tool, it shouldn't be dismissed as an elementary concept. That is, once you've run one or two questioned activities through a checklist of biblical principles, you may get the feeling that from now on—with your fresh enlightenment—you can just go back to the old be-nudged-in-the-right-direction-by-the-Spirit system of ethics. But don't give in to the feeling, OK?

Why? Let me explain it this way. In years past, our spiritual forefathers, unencumbered by the illusions of a "Christian" society, saw the need to hammer out for themselves the basics of living according to biblical scruples. Plowing through the Word, they would come to certain conclusions during that period of history as to what was right or wrong in the sight of God. They handed these conclusions down through the generations as the rights and wrongs of the Bible.

But the world changed—the environment in which the conclusions had been formed was expanding, altering—and new conclusions were needed. Our "fathers" had passed on *their* conclusions; yet somewhere down the line in the 20th century, *we* seem to have forgotten the process of how they *arrived* at their conclusions of right and wrong. We've missed the whole point of righteous Christian living: the key lies not in historical conclusions but in eternal principles.

Now we've got to get used to not missing the point for a while. The idea is to exercise our use of the process of determining right/wrong. A checklist is not *the* answer—it's simply a lesson in how to start *using* biblical principles. So hang on a little longer to the checklist idea!

2. *Universal Conclusions?*　　Here's a hefty area of concern which may have crossed your mind. Do rights and wrongs differ with cultures? Do rights and wrongs differ with individual believers? The answer is yes. Before you moan that here's just another ethical system of "relativity," think with me.

Have you ever been confronted with the question of why does it seem all right for the typical European Christian to sip wine at a meal when the practice is frowned on in the United States? Or why were ladies' bare ankles so risqué to the Christian of 1900, when now the exposure of a shinbone isn't even *considered* in a right/wrong list of Christian propriety? Well-versed in the now-sophisticated

school of Christian cynicism, a speaker once re-
marked, "The Christian standard for what's right to
wear is, if it's dated by three years, you're *right
on!*" Why do our moral judgments change? Do
God's ideas of right and wrong change?

Let's make it simple. I'm a pizza lover. I admit
it without shame. As a born-again, Spirit-controlled
believer, I can run the question of "Should I engage
in devouring a pepperoni pizza tonight after the
football game?" through a checklist of biblical principles and decide that it would be all right. It would
not be wrong.

But let a friend of mine who has gastric ulcers
run the question through a checklist of biblical principles. His doctor has informed him that if he par-
takes of spicy foods, he'll be further injuring his
body. He too is a born-again, Spirit-controlled believer; and yet his checklist process would reveal
at least one "minus," following the principle regarding the care of our bodies as the temple of the
Holy Spirit (1 Cor. 3:17; 6:19). For him, the pepperoni pizza would not be in line with the best
possible life. He wouldn't be "loving" his body
properly. The activity would be wrong. Wrong for
him, and yet right for me.

Did God's idea of right/wrong change? Of course
not—His concept of "right" always was, is, and will
be hinged on the fact that a Christian's body is
God's temple. The principle is eternal and thus always applicable. The biblical system or process of
using the eternal principle is likewise a constant.
So the only variable in this whole situation lies in
the *application* of scriptural principles. The principles are solid, unchanging from culture to culture
or century to century. But the applications, the conclusions reached by using the eternal principles,

can change! Another example might help to establish the validity of this.

A Bible narrative describes the "leaping and dancing" of King David as the Ark of the Covenant was being returned to the capitol (2 Sam. 6:12-23). David's dancing seems to have been an acceptable thing—notice David's rebuke of his wife Michal's criticism. But why, then, has dancing usually been put down so haughtily in most solidly biblical Christian circles in our century? Let's interview David; then we'll ask the 1933 Miss Dance Marathon of America the same questions.

"Excuse me, King David. I, uh, notice you're leaping and dancing here in front of the procession carrying the Ark. Do you, uh, usually dance like this?"

"Oh, every once in a while. When I want to praise the Lord."

"Well, certainly. Listen, King David, may I ask you a series of questions on all this? Would you mind?"

(Puff, puff.) "Not at all."

"Is this activity slowing you down in becoming more like God Himself?"

"No."

"Is it useful?"

"Yep."

"Is the Lord in control of your thoughts and emotions and body right now?"

"He is."

"Is this a good example of how to act for your people?"

"Is praising the Lord a good example? What kind of a question is that? And who are you, anyhow?"

And we could go on with the interview, covering as many of the basic principles of the Bible as time allowed. The answers would probably be consistently in harmony with the principles of Scripture; and we'd find that David's "dancing before the Lord" in his period of history, in his society, in his individual life, was a good thing. It was right. OK?

Now for our exclusive interview with Miss Dance Marathon of America—1933 (who happens to be a born-again believer):

"Excuse me, Miss Marathon. I, uh, notice that you're leaping and dancing here in front of the civic auditorium housing this event. Do you, uh, usually dance like this?"

"Oh, every once in a while. When I want to really get into it. Easy way to earn a few bucks if I can hang on for a day or two—won first place for dancing 28 hours straight last month."

"Well, certainly. Listen, Miss Marathon, may I ask you a series of questions on all this? Would you mind?"

(Puff, puff.) "Not at all."

"Is this activity slowing you down in becoming more like Christ Himself?"

"What? Well, I guess it's not exactly speeding me up, right Buster?"

"Is it useful?"

"Useful? That's not the point of dancing at all. What is this, anyway?"

"Is the Lord in control of your thoughts and emotions and body right now?"

"Your guess is as good as mine, Buddy."

"Is this a good example of how to act for other Christians?"

"Oh, come on. Get off my back, will ya? And who are you, anyway?"

So we could go on with the interview, making the poor kid more defensive as we went. The dancer might sense more and more pressure from the principles of Scripture; and *if* a "minus" resulted in just one area of the checklist, the activity in 1933, in her society, in the individual life of the dancer, is not a good thing, it would be wrong, while the same activity was right for King David!

You notice that I'm not stating that The Official Rule for All Christians in America Today is "Thou shalt not dance." Did you notice that? What I am stating is that if the dancer's answers were like those in the interview, it is likely that dancing would be wrong in her personal case. The reason that I cannot proclaim a universal decree against dancing for Christendom is because the application of biblical principles can vary from culture to culture and from time to time. That is, the conclusions of right and wrong which are reached can actually vary; even though the same Spirit gives wisdom and guidance, and even though the same biblical principles are consulted.

Where the Bible is not explicit in what we're calling these "gray areas," different circumstantial input (period of history, opinion of society, person involved, etc.) can biblically produce different conclusions. I certainly shouldn't feel obligated to coerce all Christians to follow *my* conclusions. Are you catching all this? It boils down to: if the Bible isn't explicit to all Christians on certain gray areas, what makes me think that *my* right/wrong applications should be explicit to all Christians?

My obligation is to proclaim the "Thus-saith-the-Lord" of Scripture soundly and to educate others in the use of biblical principles, *not* to dictate *my* gray-area conclusions of right or wrong as the Universal Ultimatums for Mankind. We need to be careful to instruct younger Christians in the solid truths of the Word, and to let the *Spirit* instruct younger Christians in the application of those truths.

3. *But What About Families?*   If we're not to enforce our gray-area conclusions of right/wrong on others, why is it that parents are commanded to set standards for their children?

The Bible is pretty handy with answers in this area. If the right/wrong conclusions of a youth should differ from the right/wrong conclusions of his parent, a commandment goes into effect which states, "Children, obey your parents" (Eph. 6:1). Parents are responsible to implement right behavior (Deut. 6:7) while the child's mechanisms for moral decision-making are developing.

There's an important point here. God expects me as a parent to give standards of right/wrong for the lives of my children, but not necessarily to give them all *my* standards from my own life. Do you see the difference?

When I'm determining my son's hair length, I'm determining *his* right hair length, not mine. When a 45-year-old mother is determining her teenage daughter's skirt-length, she's not determining a middle-aged standard but one biblically right for an adolescent. While most standards will be the same for parent and child (such as not hurting the body with harmful foods), some will vary. A lot of recreation time for a child would be fine while the same amount would be wasteful for a parent! So parents *are* to set right/wrong standards for the lives of their children.

Does this mean that every conclusion a parent comes to is exactly, consistently right? Impossible! (1 John 1:8) There are those who are zealous to restore a sense of parental authority in the wake of confusing right/wrong standards, and we *do* need to recognize again that God's will can be revealed through parents, that God actually can shape the life of a child through parents' direction.

However, if we stretch the biblical idea of parental authority too far, we begin thinking that God's will for a life is the parents' will. And that every direction of parents—every right/wrong conclusion—is authored by God Himself. And that a child should become what his parents want him to be as a sign of his submission under God. These are dangerous insinuations, especially in the light of the fact that parents can be totally opposed to all that true Christianity represents.

God's will is for children to obey parents. God's will is not necessarily expressed in each parental directive. God wants children to obey for obedience' sake, not because parents' conclusions are always right. God's ultimate will for a child's life may or may not be shared by parents. Often I see youth whose parents have established the vocational route of their children's lives, when the children themselves sense God's call in another direction.

Even in these situations, "Children, obey your parents" is in strict operation. As long as our parents' directives don't violate Scripture we are to do —in the right attitude—what our parents direct us to do. We are not *necessarily* to be what our parents want us to be, however; we are to be expressly what God wants us to be.

To clarify any misunderstanding at this delicate point, let's summarize the effect of Ephesians 6:1. Without rationalization, without fanfare, without a squabble—children and youth are to obey the dictates and follow the conclusions of their parents. And this set-up is in effect until the youth establishes his own independent household, when father and mother are no longer his "parents" (in the literal sense of "one who brings into becoming," one who helps develop the child to adulthood).

Even then, though, children are to "honor your father and mother" (Ex. 20:12; Deut. 5:16; Matt. 15:4; 19:19; Mark 7:10; 10:19; Luke 18:20; Eph. 6:2).

Parents are divinely responsible for the spiritual upbringing and welfare of their children, so the youth's maxim to obey his parents' right/wrong conclusions is a necessity during those years of development, God-designed for the sake of control. Let me illustrate.

My father just loves barber shops. He likes haircuts. And he like haircuts involving the barber nearly scraping off skin as he straight-razors around the ears. Being one who is not quite so fond of the barbershop routine, I was often close to the brink of spiritual heathendom in my dad's estimation. But in that subtle attitude which says "I don't necessarily agree with you but I want to respectfully and lovingly obey you," I learned to obey my parents even in that temperamental area.

The fact that I was a clean-cut kid does not necessarily mean that God's dictum for mankind is for all males to have hair extending no more than one inch from the scalp. My all-American visage *did* mean that I was following God's overall command to children to obey parents; my parents just happened to be the ones who loved crew cuts. Now when I travel to visit my parents, in a good exercise in humility, I make a visit to the barbershop beforehand in order to *honor* my parents.

"Obey your parents" creates a huge area of responsibility for both parents and kids, but it should not be an excuse for parents' failure to put out the effort to communicate reasons for right/wrong conclusions. And it doesn't excuse young people from seeking to develop right/wrong convictions of their own.

4. *Why a List?*   If a single principle applies in a situation, why bother with a whole *list* of principles in determining right or wrong? The answer lies in the lamentable fact that we're pretty stupid sometimes. When *we* think we can reach a definite conclusion of right or wrong by regarding just one principle, we may not be seeing all there is to see as we fit the situation to the biblical principle. Let's take a "for instance."

Mrs. Schwartz wonders whether it would be good or bad, right or wrong, for her darling daughter Diana to invite Harold, a non-Christian, over for a homework session. Mrs. Schwartz, remembering 2 Corinthians 6:14 ("Do not be bound together with unbelievers; for what partnership have righteousness and lawlessness, or what fellowship has light with darkness?") begins to tell Diana that she is not to be "unequally yoked."

Diana responds emphatically that inviting brainy Harold over to do homework is not being "yoked."

Then Mrs. Schwartz suggests to Diana that this could be just the beginning of a relationship which could lead even to marriage.

To which Diana replies that Harold is homely and has a personality like wet bread and is of no romantic interest to her.

On and on it goes.

The whole discussion could have been simpler, more biblically oriented, and more conclusive if mother and daughter would have considered a list of principles rather than a single principle. The one principle *did* apply, but its fuzziness in this particular application (who is to say just *how* yoked is "yoked"?) is clarified when subjected to others of God's principles. Mrs. Schwartz and daughter Diana could have considered whether the proposed activity would violate the principle of Excess (will Harold's visit impede Diana's spiritual growth?), or Emulation (is it a Christ-like mannerism to informally meet with an unbeliever?), or others.

Or the conflict could have been between Mr. Schwartz and his sloppy son Sigmund over how long the boy's hair should be. The scriptural statement is easily acknowledged: it is a shame for a man to have long hair (see 1 Cor. 11:14-15). But as every Christian father and teenage son know, the real hassle is over "how long is 'long'?" Even this can be answered in a definite way by acknowledging *other* basic principles of Christian conduct for Sigmund's life: As an isolated consideration, does what grows on Sig's head affect his spiritual growth —his race to become like Christ? Is it useful or wasteful? Is it a factor in his witness to his world? And so on.

The principles overlap in application, so when a clear conclusion can't be reached through the use of a single principle, other principles will bring the rightness or wrongness of an activity into focus.

And that's the reason for the number of principles in the Word—because we're still fallible in figuring out how an isolated principle can apply. Basically, the only principles we would need if we could match the exact thought processes of the mind of God are (1) Love the Lord your God, (2) love your neighbor, and (3) love yourself properly (Matt. 22:37-39). Unfortunately, most of us have a tough time trying to match the exact thought processes of God. Thus the *list* of principles.

More Principles

So let's get back to the principles for a moment and mention several more of the basic ones:

Leviticus 19:18	REVENGE: I am not to avenge myself.
Matthew 18:21-22	FORGIVENESS: I am always to be forgiving.
Luke 12:37-48	STEWARDSHIP: I am to be a faithful manager of what God entrusts to me.
Romans 12:2	CONFORMITY: I am not to conform to this Satanically run world.
Romans 12:10	PREFERENCE: I am to put others' welfare before my own.
Romans 12:18	PEACE: As much as possible, I am to be at peace with all men.
Romans 13:1	SUBJECTION: I am to be in subjection to governing authorities. The *only* exception to this is if my government or any authority specifically orders me to disobey the Word of God (Acts 4:13-20).
Galatians 6:10	GOODNESS: I am to do good to all men.
1 Corinthians 6:19	BODY: My body and everything in it is God's temple; it belongs to Him. I am to treat it accordingly.

2 Corinthians 6:14	YOKE: I am not to be intimately tied together with unbelievers.
1 Thessalonians 5:22	APPEARANCE: I am to avoid every form of evil.
2 Timothy 2:22	LUST: I am to run—figuratively or even literally—from youthful lusts.

And we could go on. As you study the Word with an eye for principles of conduct (and you *do* realize that is *your* responsibility, not some little book's), more and more will become evident and you can add to the list. But for now, let's attempt one more series where we use a checklist of biblical principles to arrive at God's direction of right or wrong for our lives.

Final Exam

Using the wisdom of the Spirit, run these activities —checking under True or False at each principle —through the following checklist. (If you feel that the suggested question doesn't apply to you, just fake it and pretend you're a person to whom the activity *could* apply. You'll be surprised at the way your "pretended" conclusions tend to provide fantastic insight into the problem areas of other people!) And remember the weakness of using a checklist such as this: it isn't a do-it-yourself exercise in Pharisaical legalism, just a checkpoint consideration of God's guidelines for living. A response of wholehearted obedience to the Lord is still the key to your enjoying His life-style.

Remember:

1. Ask the Spirit for wisdom and guidance.

2. If really neither true nor false, leave a blank at that slot.

3. If you disagree with the conclusion, it's your problem—not God's.

4. The conclusion is *your* personal conclusion. Don't be so dogmatic as to force the rest of us to agree exactly with what God has decided for *you!*

Fill out the charts on pages 89-94 using the wisdom of the Spirit.

In Summary

Are the possibilities getting more exciting as you accustom yourself to considering God's ideas of what's right and what isn't? The main thoughts in this whole area, again, rest on the fact that God knows right from wrong and He wants man to live according to what is best. If I am living in line with what He says is right, that means I am living a God-designed life—not in a grandly mystical way but in the practical nitty-gritties of earthly reality. And a God-designed life is the best possible life—a life of right living, and a life of right loving in the three dimensions of relationship: with God, others, and self.

The commands of the Bible treat many specific questions of conduct, and the pattern of principles in the Bible covers whatever is left in the realm of possible human activity. The application and usage of these principles, then, is the key to dealing with the "gray areas" of right and wrong.

As a simplified start in the right direction, our study together demands that you go on from here. It's with the personal reevaluation and reinstitution of the biblical system that once again the people of God can be setting the standards of conduct in society, repairing the fissures of moral and ethical absurdity in our corporate way of life by responding to the Spirit's injunction: "I solemnly charge you in the presence of God and of Christ Jesus and of His chosen angels, to maintain these principles without bias" (1 Tim. 5:21).

So let's maintain some principles, all right? And maybe I can begin spending a few less youth minister mornings on the phone trying to comfort victims of this whole right/wrong confusion.

A. Is it right or wrong for me to drink coffee?

REFERENCE	PRINCIPLE	TRUE	FALSE
Heb. 12:1	EXCESS: It doesn't slow me down spiritually		
1 Cor. 6:12	EXPEDIENCE: It can be profitable, useful		
1 Cor. 6:12	ENSLAVEMENT: I can be Spirit-controlled in this		
Rom. 14:13	EXAMPLE: It can allow me to be a good example		
Col. 4:5	EVANGELISM: It can help spread the Gospel		
1 Cor. 10:23	EDIFICATION: It can help other Christians		
1 Cor. 10:31	EXALTATION: It can glorify God		
1 John 2:6	EMULATION: I can imitate Christ in this		
Lev. 19:18	REVENGE: It has nothing to do with avenging myself		
Matt.18:21-22	FORGIVENESS: I can demonstrate forgiveness in this		
Luke 12:37-48	STEWARDSHIP: I can be a good steward in this		
Rom. 12:2	CONFORMITY: This won't conform me to Satan's world		
Rom. 12:10	PREFERENCE: I can put others before me in this		
Rom. 12:18	PEACE: I can maintain peace with others in this		
Rom. 13:1	SUBJECTION: It can show my subjection to authority		
Gal. 6:10	GOODNESS: I can show goodness to others in this		
1 Cor. 6:19	BODY· This doesn't harm God's temple in any way		
2 Cor. 6:14	YOKE: This won't bind me to unbelievers		
1 Thes. 5:22	APPEARANCE: I'm free from evil appearance in this		
2 Tim. 2:22	LUST: I'm free from any chance to lust in this		

THEREFORE, FOR ME, DRINKING COFFEE IS: ___RIGHT ___WRONG

B. Is it right or wrong for me to wear the same style clothes as my non-Christian friends?

REFERENCE	PRINCIPLE	TRUE	FALSE
Heb. 12:1	EXCESS: It doesn't slow me down spiritually		
1 Cor. 6:12	EXPEDIENCE: It can be profitable, useful		
1 Cor. 6:12	ENSLAVEMENT: I can be Spirit-controlled in this		
Rom. 14:13	EXAMPLE: It can allow me to be a good example		
Col. 4:5	EVANGELISM: It can help spread the Gospel		
1 Cor. 10:23	EDIFICATION: It can help other Christians		
1 Cor. 10:31	EXALTATION: It can glorify God		
1 John 2:6	EMULATION: I can imitate Christ in this		
Lev. 19:18	REVENGE: It has nothing to do with avenging myself		
Matt.18:21-22	FORGIVENESS: I can demonstrate forgiveness in this		
Luke 12:37-48	STEWARDSHIP: I can be a good steward in this		
Rom. 12:2	CONFORMITY: This won't conform me to Satan's world		
Rom. 12:10	PREFERENCE: I can put others before me in this		
Rom. 12:18	PEACE: I can maintain peace with others in this		
Rom. 13:1	SUBJECTION: It can show my subjection to authority		
Gal. 6:10	GOODNESS: I can show goodness to others in this		
1 Cor. 6:19	BODY: This doesn't harm God's temple in any way		
2 Cor. 6:14	YOKE: This won't bind me to unbelievers		
1 Thes. 5:22	APPEARANCE: I'm free from evil appearance in this		
2 Tim. 2:22	LUST: I'm free from any chance to lust in this		

THEREFORE, WEARING STYLISH CLOTHES IS: ___RIGHT ___WRONG

C. Is it right or wrong for me to marry someone of another race?

REFERENCE	PRINCIPLE	TRUE	FALSE
Heb. 12:1	EXCESS: It doesn't slow me down spiritually		
1 Cor. 6:12	EXPEDIENCE: It can be profitable, useful		
1 Cor. 6:12	ENSLAVEMENT: I can be Spirit-controlled in this		
Rom. 14:13	EXAMPLE: It can allow me to be a good example		
Col. 4:5	EVANGELISM: It can help spread the Gospel		
1 Cor. 10:23	EDIFICATION: It can help other Christians		
1 Cor. 10:31	EXALTATION: It can glorify God		
1 John 2:6	EMULATION: I can imitate Christ in this		
Lev. 19:18	REVENGE: It has nothing to do with avenging myself		
Matt.18:21-22	FORGIVENESS: I can demonstrate forgiveness in this		
Luke 12:37-48	STEWARDSHIP: I can be a good steward in this		
Rom. 12:2	CONFORMITY: This won't conform me to Satan's world		
Rom. 12:10	PREFERENCE: I can put others before me in this		
Rom. 12:18	PEACE: I can maintain peace with others in this		
Rom. 13:1	SUBJECTION: It can show my subjection to authority		
Gal. 6:10	GOODNESS: I can show goodness to others in this		
1 Cor. 6:19	BODY: This doesn't harm God's temple in any way		
2 Cor. 6:14	YOKE: This won't bind me to unbelievers		
1 Thes. 5:22	APPEARANCE: I'm free from evil appearance in this		
2 Tim. 2:22	LUST: I'm free from any chance to lust in this		

THEREFORE, MARRYING SOMEONE OF ANOTHER RACE IS . . .
___RIGHT ___WRONG

D. Is it right or wrong for me occasionally to drink a little wine?

REFERENCE	PRINCIPLE	TRUE	FALSE
Heb. 12:1	EXCESS: It doesn't slow me down spiritually		
1 Cor. 6:12	EXPEDIENCE: It can be profitable, useful		
1 Cor. 6:12	ENSLAVEMENT: I can be Spirit-controlled in this		
Rom. 14:13	EXAMPLE: It can allow me to be a good example		
Col. 4:5	EVANGELISM: It can help spread the Gospel		
1 Cor. 10:23	EDIFICATION: It can help other Christians		
1 Cor. 10:31	EXALTATION: It can glorify God		
1 John 2:6	EMULATION: I can imitate Christ in this		
Lev. 19:18	REVENGE: It has nothing to do with avenging myself		
Matt.18:21-22	FORGIVENESS: I can demonstrate forgiveness in this		
Luke 12:37-48	STEWARDSHIP: I can be a good steward in this		
Rom. 12:2	CONFORMITY: This won't conform me to Satan's world		
Rom. 12:10	PREFERENCE: I can put others before me in this		
Rom. 12:18	PEACE: I can maintain peace with others in this		
Rom. 13:1	SUBJECTION: It can show my subjection to authority		
Gal. 6:10	GOODNESS: I can show goodness to others in this		
1 Cor. 6:19	BODY: This doesn't harm God's temple in any way		
2 Cor. 6:14	YOKE: This won't bind me to unbelievers		
1 Thes. 5:22	APPEARANCE: I'm free from evil appearance in this		
2 Tim. 2:22	LUST: I'm free from any chance to lust in this		

THEREFORE, TO DRINK A LITTLE WINE IS . . . ___RIGHT ___WRONG

E. Your own question of right/wrong.

REFERENCE	PRINCIPLE	TRUE	FALSE
Heb. 12:1	EXCESS: It doesn't slow me down spiritually		
1 Cor. 6:12	EXPEDIENCE: It can be profitable, useful		
1 Cor. 6:12	ENSLAVEMENT: I can be Spirit-controlled in this		
Rom. 14:13	EXAMPLE: It can allow me to be a good example		
Col. 4:5	EVANGELISM: It can help spread the Gospel		
1 Cor. 10:23	EDIFICATION: It can help other Christians		
1 Cor. 10:31	EXALTATION: It can glorify God		
1 John 2:6	EMULATION: I can imitate Christ in this		
Lev. 19:18	REVENGE: It has nothing to do with avenging myself		
Matt.18:21-22	FORGIVENESS: I can demonstrate forgiveness in this		
Luke 12:37-48	STEWARDSHIP: I can be a good steward in this		
Rom. 12:2	CONFORMITY: This won't conform me to Satan's world		
Rom. 12:10	PREFERENCE: I can put others before me in this		
Rom. 12:18	PEACE: I can maintain peace with others in this		
Rom. 13:1	SUBJECTION: It can show my subjection to authority		
Gal. 6:10	GOODNESS: I can show goodness to others in this		
1 Cor. 6:19	BODY: This doesn't harm God's temple in any way		
2 Cor. 6:14	YOKE: This won't bind me to unbelievers		
1 Thes. 5:22	APPEARANCE: I'm free from evil appearance in this		
2 Tim. 2:22	LUST: I'm free from any chance to lust in this		

THEREFORE, MY QUESTIONED ACTIVITY IS . . . ___RIGHT ___WRONG

F. Your own question of right/wrong.

REFERENCE	PRINCIPLE	TRUE	FALSE
Heb. 12:1	EXCESS: It doesn't slow me down spiritually		
1 Cor. 6:12	EXPEDIENCE: It can be profitable, useful		
1 Cor. 6:12	ENSLAVEMENT: I can be Spirit-controlled in this		
Rom. 14:13	EXAMPLE: It can allow me to be a good example		
Col. 4:5	EVANGELISM: It can help spread the Gospel		
1 Cor. 10:23	EDIFICATION: It can help other Christians		
1 Cor. 10:31	EXALTATION: It can glorify God		
1 John 2:6	EMULATION: I can imitate Christ in this		
Lev. 19:18	REVENGE: It has nothing to do with avenging myself		
Matt.18:21-22	FORGIVENESS: I can demonstrate forgiveness in this		
Luke 12:37-48	STEWARDSHIP: I can be a good steward in this		
Rom. 12:2	CONFORMITY: This won't conform me to Satan's world		
Rom. 12:10	PREFERENCE: I can put others before me in this		
Rom. 12:18	PEACE: I can maintain peace with others in this		
Rom. 13:1	SUBJECTION: It can show my subjection to authority		
Gal. 6:10	GOODNESS: I can show goodness to others in this		
1 Cor. 6:19	BODY: This doesn't harm God's temple in any way		
2 Cor. 6:14	YOKE: This won't bind me to unbelievers		
1 Thes. 5:22	APPEARANCE: I'm free from evil appearance in this		
2 Tim. 2:22	LUST: I'm free from any chance to lust in this		

THEREFORE, MY QUESTIONED ACTIVITY IS . . . ___RIGHT ___WRONG